The Ninth Karmapa, Wangchuk Dorje's

Ocean of Certainty

The Ninth Karmapa, Wangchuk Dorje's

Ocean of Certainty

Commentary by Traleg Kyabgon

KTD Publications
Woodstock, New York

Published by KTD Publications
335 Meads Mountain Road
Woodstock, New York 12498

Pith Instructions of Coemergent Wisdom, Entitled the Profound Essence of the Ocean of Certainty by the Ninth Karmapa, Wangchuk Dorje
Oral commentary by Traleg Kyabgon Rinpoche

These teachings on the *Pith Instructions of Coemergent Wisdom* were given by Traleg Kyabgon at E-Vam Buddhist Institute, Melbourne, 1993.

For further information please contact:
E-Vam Institute in New York
171 Water Street
Chatham, New York 12037
Tel: 518-392-6900
www.evam.org

ISBN: 978-1-934608-20-3

Text layout by BasiaDesign
www.basia-design.com

Printed in the USA on 100% PCR, acid-free paper.

Contents

Traleg Kyabgon Rinpoche, E-Vam Institute, Chatham NY, 2009

Traleg Kyabgon
A Short Biography

Traleg Kyabgon Rinpoche was born in 1955 in Eastern Tibet. At age two, he was recognized by His Holiness the sixteenth Gyalwang Karmapa, head of the Kagyu lineage, as the ninth incarnation of the Traleg tulkus, which can be traced back to the time of Saltong Shogam, a contemporary of the first Karmapa. Traleg Rinpoche was enthroned as the Abbot of Thrangu Monastery in Tibet and following the Chinese invasion of his country was taken to safety in India. There he continued the rigorous training prescribed for tulkus born with responsibilities as major lineage holders in the Tibetan tradition of Vajrayana Buddhism. This training included five years at Sanskrit University in Varanasi and several years at Rumtek Monastery, the main seat of the Karma Kagyu Lineage. Not only has Traleg Rinpoche received the complete teachings of the Karma Kagyu tradition of Vajrayana Buddhism, but he is also well acquainted with the practices and philosophy of the Drugpa Kagyu strand of the Kagyu lineage, having spent nine years studying with the Regent of the Drugpa Kagyu, the late Dungse Rinpoche, at his monastery in Darjeeling.

Rinpoche settled in Australia in 1980 in order to make the teachings and practices of the Kagyu tradition available there. He established the Kagyu E-Vam Buddhist Institute in Melbourne, Australia in 1982, Maitripa Contemplative Center in Healesville, Victoria in 1997, Nyima Tashi in Auckland, New Zealand in 1999, and Yeshe Nyima in Sydney, Australia in 2008. Rinpoche has been traveling and teaching in the United States since 1988 and established E-Vam Institute in Chatham, New York in 2005. Rinpoche also travels widely, giving lectures and seminars on Buddhism and related topics in Europe, Canada, New Zealand, and Southeast Asia.

The Ninth Karmapa, Wangchuk Dorje's

Ocean of Certainty

Introduction

Traleg Kyabgon

I supplicate the guru, the embodiment of Vajradhara
To dwell inseparably above my head.
With that, I would like to set out my intention,
To write about the precious teachings of the
Kagyu lineage,
In a text entitled the *Profound Essence of the
Ocean of Certainty.*

The realizations of impermanence and the inevitability of death act as the motivating factor for meditators to realize the depths of suffering in samsara. They will then abandon all concern with temporal matters and give thoughts to the welfare of all sentient beings, who have been their own mother and father in previous lives, and aspire to attain enlightenment for their benefit. They may even want to achieve enlightenment in one lifetime and with a single body through the effective methods of vajrayana. We can only praise such people for their sincere desire and interest in learning the profound and essential pith instructions. To understand the pith instructions properly, we must first understand our own psychological predilections. We cannot release the arrow if we do not see the target.

Before embarking on the spiritual path, you must realize, right from the beginning, that all living beings are sooner or later bound to die. Suffering is ever-present in the human condition because of this inevitability of death and change. Sentient beings wander from one form of existence to another in the six realms of the samsaric condition. Having understood that all beings who wander in samsara experience enormous suffering, you should develop the wish to attain enlightenment to alleviate their various sufferings. The best method for achieving enlightenment in one lifetime is the tantrayana, because that is the most expedient for achieving enlightenment quickly.

Some people may embark on the spiritual path to avoid undesirable forms of existence in the next life rather than to attain enlightenment. That may be good, but such people still need to undertake certain spiritual practices to ensure a better form of rebirth. However, this is not the best way to approach spirituality. We should take into account the different personalities and predilections of such people or it will be difficult to offer them suitable advice. This would be comparable to releasing an arrow without seeing the target or to shooting an arrow into the dark. Even people with a degree of training in meditation should not rely completely on their own understanding and familiarity with the practice and feel it is sufficient. The same thing can be said of people who have spent a great deal of time improving their understanding of Buddhist philosophy. Such intellectual understanding is also insufficient because we need to translate intellectual understanding into direct experience.

Having made these points, it can be said clearly and simply, the spiritual advice offered in this text will not involve many philosophical references. I will extract the essence of the teachings, as contained in various texts and commentaries, and present it in a way that is not contaminated by philosophical arguments or the use of antidotes. It will simply relate to your immediate direct experiences.

According to the Kagyupa masters, it is extremely important to offer spiritual advice by taking the needs of different individuals into account, so we have different lineages coming from different sources, but all these streams are united within the Kagyu tradition. We have the mahamudra lineage, which was passed down from Milarepa to Gampopa and so on and which emphasize the teaching of the so-called "sudden path" of mahamudra. There is also the lineage of the Kadampa tradition, which originates with Gampopa himself, as he was a Kadampa master before becoming a disciple of Milarepa. This teaching emphasizes the *lam-rim* or "path and stages" of the gradual approach. The Kadampa lineage is also divided into three main streams: the "lineage of vast action" or the Yogacara School, the "lineage of profound view" or the Madhyamaka School, and the "lineage of direct experience," which involves the transference of experience from master to disciple. The last lineage is the most important, and was transmitted from Tilopa to Naropa and then down through the different generations of Kagyu masters.

Generally speaking, the Buddhist teachings are presented in the three yana format of hinayana, mahayana, and vajrayana. These yanas are taught in accordance with three different types of human beings, and through them, human beings are able to move from one spiritual level to another until they eventually attain enlightenment. The way the paths and stages are formulated is varied and complicated. However, at this point, it is not necessary to know all the subtle distinctions between them. What is essential is to realize sentient beings caught in the samsaric condition endure immense suffering and that it is essential to remove that suffering. Try to develop the impetus to achieve enlightenment for this reason. You should not wish to achieve enlightenment at some indeterminate time in the future either but to attain it in this very lifetime.

According to the traditional teachings, anyone who develops this attitude belongs to the spiritual family of the mahayana and possesses supreme intelligence. However, it should be emphasized that this is not always the case. There may be people who are not completely ripe for the mahayana teachings, but who through good companionship and contact with appropriate teachings, can be spiritually ripened and become a proper vessel to receive and contain the teachings of the mahayana. Before the proper teachings are received and practiced, it is important to ascertain that the vessel is devoid of any faults or defects and can contain whatever is poured into it. The way to ensure this is by practicing the *ngondro* or "preliminary practices." You become a proper vessel by engaging in the preliminary practices and you will then be able to contain the teachings subsequent to that.

The ngondro teachings are practiced step by step as we go through different stages of realization. These correspond to the *Four Dharmas of Gampopa*, which lays out a gradual progression of attainments and realizations. It is important not to skip any steps. Do the initial practices first and the later practices later and not the other way around. When preparing to receive spiritual instructions and advice, it is important to avoid certain shortcomings, such as laziness, distraction, or fixation on sensory impressions. The ngondro practices help to ensure that obstacles do not arise. All practices in the Buddhist teachings consist of three parts—the preliminaries, the actual body of practice, and the conclusion—and they must be practiced in this order.

There are two types of preliminaries: the ordinary preliminary practices and the extraordinary preliminary practices.

The Preliminaries

The Four Ordinary Preliminaries

The ordinary preliminary practices consist of four contemplations:

The precious human body
Death and impermanence
The infallibility of karmic cause and effect
The dissatisfactory nature of samsara

The Precious Human Body

The first topic is the difficulty of obtaining a precious human rebirth. It is not easy to obtain a human body, but only by doing so can we can aspire toward higher spiritual goals. This attainment is also the way to become free from physical labor and to gain leisure. The "precious human body" is *dal 'byor* in Tibetan. *Dal ba* means "leisure," because only human beings have the leisure to orient their lives toward spiritual goals and *'byor ba* means "attainment," because human beings have the opportunity to make use of this body to achieve their desired goals. This is not possible for any other kind of living being.

Dal 'byor can also be interpreted slightly differently because *dal ba* also means "the human body possesses eight different kinds of leisure." These are: 1) not being born in the hell realms, 2) not being born in the hungry ghost realms, 3) not being born in the animal realms, 4) not being born in the god realms, 5) not being born as a savage, 6) not being born with wrong views, 7) not being born in an environment with no spirituality, and 8) not being born with intellectual or physical disabilities.

'Byor ba can also be interpreted to mean, "there are ten kinds of attainments." These are: 1) being born a human being, 2) being born in a center of vibrant spiritual activities, 3) being free from any mental or physical disability, 4) being born in an environment where you are not misled into holding dogmatic and wrong views about spirituality, and 5) having an inclination toward spiritual practices. These are called "the five attainments in relation to oneself." Then there are: 6) being born in an environment where enlightened beings have set foot, 7) being born in an environment where enlightened beings have given teachings and spiritual guidance, 8) being born in a place with a living tradition, 9) being born in an environment where that tradition is perpetuated by devoted followers, and 10) having compassion towards others and the desire to alleviate their suffering. These are called "the five attainments in relation to the environment."

Someone in possession of the eight leisures and the ten attainments has a precious human body. It is called "precious" for two reasons: the human body is so difficult to obtain, and it can be used for various benefits. It is therefore comparable to a precious gem. In addition, to be in possession of a human body and have the opportunity to practice the tantric teachings is extremely rare. To be in possession of this body and to have that opportunity does not come about through an accident of nature—it is the result of our own past deeds. You must understand that this good circumstance has arisen because of your own positive deeds in the past.

When you contemplate the difficulty of obtaining

a precious human body, you should look at other forms of life and see how many nonhuman forms there are compared to the number of human beings. You will then realize the number of human beings is comparably very small. Shantideva's *Bodhicharyavatara* says:

> Imagine a yoke adrift on the surface of the sea
> And a one-eyed turtle who surfaces every
> hundred years
> That perchance can place his head through that
> yoke;
> The chance of being born a human is even smaller!

Chandragomin also says:

> The human body is difficult to obtain,
> But once you have obtained it,
> You can make use of it for various purposes.
> It is possible to attain enlightenment as
> a consequence.

The *Bodhisattvapitaka sutra* says:

> To obtain human birth is difficult,
> To preserve your life is difficult,
> To receive proper spiritual guidance is difficult,
> And to attain enlightenment is difficult.

The *Karunapundarika sutra* says:

> To obtain a human birth is difficult.
> Even if you are born a human being,
> It is difficult to possess the necessary faculties.
> It is difficult to live in a proper environment,
> And very difficult to be born in a vibrant
> spiritual tradition.

> Even if you are born in such a tradition,
> It is very difficult to respond appropriately.
> It is also very difficult to develop the right kind of aspiration.

Many comments such as this can be cited from the sutras.

Having understood the difficulty of obtaining this human body, you should develop the right attitude toward it. You should see your human body as a vehicle, a ship, a horse or a servant. You can be transported from one state of being to another if you rely on this body. By relying on the ship of your body, you will be able to cross the ocean of samsara, so instead of wasting your body or misusing it, use it for creating wholesome karma. Shantideva's *Bodhicharyavatara* says:

> You should cross the ocean of suffering,
> By relying on the ship of the human body.
> You may not be able to find such a ship again;
> So deluded ones; awaken from your slumber!

It also says:

> The precious human body is like a horse
> Which you should ride to cross the dangerous gorge of suffering.

Just being born a human being does not in itself qualify as a "precious" human birth. Someone may appear to be in the possession of a body completely free from any defects, but as far as that person's inner life is concerned, it is void of spirituality. Such a person is barren, almost like an animal pretending to be a human being or emulating human behavior. However, if a person is rich within and has a mind filled with humility and spiritual inspirations, then regardless of their physical defects, they have obtained the precious human body. Even if the body is sound, an impoverished inner mental life will prevent someone making proper use of the body, and as a consequence, the attainment of buddhahood will only be a remote possibility for them. The *Buddhavatamsaka sutra* says:

> Someone devoid of inner spiritual vitality
> Will never give birth to the wholesome spiritual qualities.

The *Dasadharmaka sutra* says:

> Just as no one would expect a sprout
> To come from a burnt seed,
> No one would expect virtue
> From a mind with no faith.

To become enriched within, it is important to develop humility and conviction. We need conviction in the infallibility of karmic cause and effect, the infallibility of truth, and the infallibility of the Triple Gem. The mind becomes lucid and free of embellishments if we develop conviction and humility. There are three aspects to conviction: 1) the conviction of nondelusion, 2) the conviction of trust, and 3) the conviction of inclination.

The conviction of nondelusion means the object of conviction is pure and does not give rise to delusions. Objects of conviction like the Buddha, Dharma, and Sangha help to remove delusions and make the mind lucid.

The conviction of trust means you have to trust in the infallibility of karmic cause and effect and believe that wholesome actions will always lead to the enjoyment of happiness, and that conversely, negative actions will automatically increase suffering.

The conviction of inclination is about developing conviction in your inclination to achieve enlightenment and to incline your mind toward that goal. The *Precious Garland* says:

> When your mind is inclined toward
> The attainment of spiritual goals,
> It should be free from hatred, fear, and ignorance.
> You will then become a proper spiritual vessel.

Do not abandon your spiritual goals by falling victim to desire, hatred, or delusions. When you develop these three types of conviction, the seed of enlightenment can be born in your mind. The *Bodhisattvapitaka sutra* says:

> Those in possession of humility and conviction,
> Become proper vessels for the Buddha's teachings
> Because they are able to comprehend those
> teachings.

Having obtained the precious human body, try to develop humility and conviction so that your actions are not wasted by indulging in unwholesome deeds or meaningless tasks of neutral significance. It is important to avoid unwholesome deeds and meaningless tasks. To do so, you must be mindful of your physical and verbal behavior and of your imperceptible mental processes. Even if you have not committed misdeeds in any apparent way, you may still entertain unwholesome thoughts, which in turn will solidify your habits and cause you more suffering in the future. Contemplate the positive qualities of your precious human body for these reasons and realize that its preciousness is what makes it so difficult to obtain and easy to lose. Your precious body is not immutable; it is fragile, and you must see the urgency of putting it to good use now.

Contemplate this until you become fully convinced of the fact you are indeed in very fortunate circumstances and should not take them for granted.

It is not sufficient to just recognize the difficulty of obtaining this precious body. You might recognize this truth but still fail to pursue spiritual goals. The pursuit of those goals is really what is at issue here. Really see the urgency of this and pursue your spiritual goals as if your hair was on fire. You must practice as diligently as if you were trying to put out that fire. Increase your learning, contemplate what you have learned, and then translate that into direct meditative experience. These three trainings are something you should protect as dearly as if you were protecting your own eyes.

The essence of this contemplation on the precious human body is twofold: 1) to understand how hard it is to obtain such a body and 2) to understand how easy it is to lose it through disease or sudden death. You should think, "From now on, I will make proper use of my human body, and no longer take it for granted." Contemplate this for as long as you need to really develop a feeling for it.

Death and Impermanence

Buddha says:

> Oh monks, all composite things are impermanent
> by nature.

If you were to wonder, "In what way are all composite things impermanent by nature?" the following citation from the *Udanavarga* says:

> The result of accumulation is exhaustion,
> The result of erecting something is falling,

> The result of meeting is separation,
> The result of birth is death.

It also says:

> Alas, all conditioned things are impermanent
> by nature,
> Because they come into existence and then
> disintegrate.

Since all composite things are subject to change, our own lives are also subject to change. You should contemplate this in relation to both the external world and the inner constitution of your body. When we observe the external world, we see continuous change that is either gradual or rapid. Time is always ticking away as the years, months, days, evenings, seconds, and moments continuously go by. The *Lalitavistara sutra* says:

> The three worlds are subject to change,
> Just like the clouds blown about in the sky.

Change is also intrinsic to the inner constitution of your body. First, you are born, then you become old, and then you die. You do not remain static for a second. Furthermore, no one can predict the length of their lives because so many different causes and conditions could bring about their demise. There is only one certainty, and that is the certainty of death itself. The *Udanavarga* says:

> Death is completely unpredictable.
> Some die in the womb,
> Some die during birth,
> Some die when they are about to crawl.
> Some die when they are old,
> But many die when they are young.

> People who are now young,
> Will gradually get old and die.

You should think, "When death comes, what will help me?" "Can anything help me at the time of death?" and "Will my wealth, reputation, and power be of any use?" Instead of helping at the time of death, those things usually just cause further suffering because of our attachment to them. Our mind is full of all kinds of worries and concerns. Not only would our wealth be useless, even our children, parents, and relatives can provide no protection for us against death. So it has been said. Contemplate impermanence and the inevitability of death in the following manner: Death is certain, but the time of death is uncertain. I will die without accomplishing all my projects and plans. All the success I have had to this point in my life will not give me the strength to face death when it arrives. Death is something real and everpresent. When I think about it, the number of people that have died is innumerable. My parents, neighbors, monastic sangha, friends, and acquaintances all made plans assuming they would live to a mature age, but in reality, many of them died before fulfilling their plans or doing the things they wanted to do in their lives.

Contemplate death in this manner and then think, "Countless human beings lived in the past but are no longer around. There are an equal number now that are still alive but will die one day. Many more human beings will be born after I have died, and they will die in due course. Death is not something that can be avoided by anyone. Even an enlightened being such as the Buddha had to die and give his body away. How much more true is it when it comes to ordinary human beings like us?" Ashvaghosha says:

> You should respond with skepticism

To anyone who talks about gods and spirits as immortal.
Even the Buddha's body—which was free from all defects
From the ordinary point of view—was subject to change.
How could anyone else
Be in possession of an everlasting body?

Think about the certainty of death, the uncertainty of the time of death, the fragility of the body and its susceptibility to life-threatening disease or poisons. Many people go to sleep healthy and do not wake up. Every day that passes and every month that passes, you are getting closer to your own death. The passage of time is quick, like the speed of an arrow, a waterfall over a cliff or a criminal approaching his execution. It is said:

The archer's arrow
Is released from the bow
And races toward its target;
Human life is just so.

The *Udanavarga* says:

When a convicted criminal
Is taken to the place of execution,
Each step he takes is one step closer to death.
Your own life is drawing closer to death in this manner.

Time is nonabiding; it does not stand still, so do not bank on the idea that you will live to fix everything in time, because you may not have that time. Many causes and conditions threaten life or bring death, but very few causes prolong life. Nagarjuna's *Suhrllekha* says:

> What we call life is threatened by various things,
> Just like a candle flickering in the wind.
> Life is as transient as bubbles in water.
> The distinction between life and death
> Is only that of an inhalation and an exhalation.
> That we actually wake up every day
> Should be a source of wonderment!

Nagarjuna's *Precious Garland* says:

> The causes and conditions
> That bring about death are numerous,
> But causes and conditions that preserve life are not
> Therefore, think of death as inevitable
> And engage in activities that will be helpful at the time of death.

The *Bodhicharyavatara* says:

> I might die before
> I have purified my negative actions.

It also says:

> It makes no sense to be happy and say,
> "At least I will not die today."
> For there will inevitably come a time
> When you no longer exist.

The essence of this second contemplation—to realize that death is certain and that the time of death is uncertain—is to realize how fortunate you are to have a precious human body with all of its faculties intact. Instead of getting caught up in various forms of dissatisfaction and discontent, it is important to develop an appreciation for what you already possess. Do not take anything for granted, thinking you will live for a long time and can take care of business sooner or later. Try to take advantage of each moment and each day as it comes and make use of that time as constructively as possible. Through contemplating death, you will make use of your time constructively, because you will see the urgency of the situation. However, if you do not properly contemplate the inevitability of death, you will not develop the impetus to use your time in a constructive fashion. You will not use it to benefit yourself and others and engage in wholesome and beneficial activities, but instead fall victim to laziness and complacency and fail to mature spiritually.

Essentially, the result of birth is death. That is certain. How and when you will die is uncertain. When the time of death comes, no thing and no one will be of any use to you. The only benefit at the time of death will be if you have used your time constructively while still alive and not wasted and misused it. If you were not able to practice the Dharma while you were alive, you will have no control over your mind at the time of death, and it will be blown about by the winds of karma.

The Infallibility of Karmic Cause and Effect

Once you have generated a genuine feeling for your mortality, you should contemplate karmic cause and effect. Karmic cause and effect is based on the experiences of pleasure and pain, happiness and suffering, because whatever we experience in life is due to the workings of karma. The *Karmashataka sutra* says:

> The varieties of karmas have created the varieties of sentient beings.

The *Abhidharmakosha-karika* says:

> All world systems have come into existence as a
> result of karma.

There are two types of karma: physical karma and mental karma. Each manifest physical action has a mental act that preceded it. Whatever we experience in terms of pain, pleasure, happiness, and suffering is the result of the things we have thought and done in the past. Every thought we entertain and every deed we perform in this life leaves a karmic impression in the mind, which will determine our future modes of existence.

There is a homogeneous relationship between cause and effect. As the following quotation says:

> If you killed in the past, your life will be short;
> If you were aggressive in the past, your life will
> never work out
> As you will encounter constant obstacles and
> difficult people;
> If you took someone's property, your life will be
> impoverished;
> If you committed adultery, you will have many
> enemies.

In any case, you have to realize that no karma we create in this life is wasted. We reap the benefit or harm of our previous deeds. Actions we may perform with excessive desire, hatred, or ignorance will propel us into an undesirable form of existence in the future. On the other hand, if we create good karma, it will propel us into wholesome modes of existence. Negative karma and the experience of suffering are intimately linked because negative karma can never produce experiences of happiness or pleasure. Conversely, positive karma directly leads to experiences of pleasure and happiness. Excessive greed and craving will lead to the realm of the hungry ghosts, extreme hatred will lead to the hell realms, and ignorance will lead to the various animal existences. The *Precious Garland* says:

> Wholesome karma leads
> To the experience of happiness.
> Unwholesome karma
> Leads to the experience of suffering.

That which is wholesome and that which is unwholesome can be determined by observing the kinds of actions that lead to happiness and the kinds of actions that lead to suffering. There are ten kinds of actions that create negative karma—three originate from the body, four originate from speech, and three originate from the mind. We should avoid these negative karmas and try to engage in positive karmas to increase our happiness.

Whether we create negative or positive karma, it all leaves an impression in the mind. These impressions are like seeds that remain dormant until the appropriate conditions trigger them again, and then they come to fruition, which results on our experiences of either happiness or suffering. It is therefore extremely important to be mindful of the way you practice on the spiritual path. Even when you engaged in religious practices, such as worship or charity, you should always look at the mental component of that action to determine your motivation. If your motivation comes from delusion, greed, craving, hatred, or pride, your actions may appear to be spiritual but they will not produce the desired results.

Furthermore, whatever karma you create, it is your own. Karma cannot be transferred from one person to another or shared by others, whether it is wholesome or unwholesome. Karmic impressions remain unconscious, and they do not disappear, even after a long time. We are each responsible for our own actions, and whatever we experience is the result of our own doing, not anybody else's. The *Surataprichcha sutra* says:

> The seeds of a chili are hot by nature,
> If you plant them, you will get hot chilies.
> If you plant fruit trees, you will get sweet fruit.
> In the same way,
> Negative karma produces the heat of negative karma
> And positive karma brings the sweetness of positive karma.

That is the way you should understand it. The *Smrtipasthana sutra* says:

> It may be possible to cool a fire,
> It may be possible to catch the wind in a noose,
> And it may be possible for the sun and moon to fall out of the sky;
> But it is not possible for the appropriate karmic results
> Not to arise from their karmic causes.

As far as karma itself is concerned, it is not certain when the results of your actions will blossom. Sometimes those results can be observed immediately. Another type of negative karma will leave an impression in the mind, but you will not experience the results until next lifetime. Yet another type of karma will be experienced many lifetimes after the fact. A fourth type of karma is indeterminate, because when we might experience its fruition is uncertain.

Sometimes the karma we create is mixed; it is not wholly negative or wholly positive. You may kill someone (which is a negative karma), but you may have done so with a positive intention (which is positive karma). For example, a sutra tells the story of a buddha who kills a ship's captain, because he knows the captain had a murderous and thieving intentions toward all the people on board. There may also be mixed karmic actions, such as practicing charity in order to perform sacrifices. These actions would bring mixed results depending on the exact combination of positive and negative karma. Karma also has to be understood in relation to *propelling karma* and *fruition karma*. Both propelling karma and fruition karma could be positive or negative.

Even in terms of positive actions, there is unsullied and sullied positive action. Sullied positive action refers to abstinence; where you might abstain from killing, stealing, and so on. Unsullied positive action refers to meditative practices, where you are purifying your mind and working toward the attainment of enlightenment.

There is also a distinction between *common karma* and *individual karma*. Common karma refers to the shared world that sentient beings live within and individual karma refers to the actions and results that we each have to experience alone as a result of our own karmic imprints.

When we realize karmic cause and effect is infallible and that what we experience is directly related to our own actions, you should make the effort to engage in what is wholesome to increase our happiness and decrease our suffering. Try to actively engage in doing what is beneficial, because it is not sufficient to just avoid harmful actions in a passive way. Actively engaging in what is wholesome and beneficial is much more important than passively abstaining from harmful deeds. Take delight in doing what is beneficial and think, "This will increase my happiness." Do what is beneficial with a sense of joy and think, "Just as a small spark can set a whole forest on fire, a small wholesome deed can eliminate an infinite number of karmic misdeeds." The *Udanavarga* says:

> Even the creation of a small wholesome deed,
> Will create enough impetus for you to get to the
>   other shore.

Avoid doing what is harmful and actively engage in what is wholesome. In addition, you should also generate bodhichitta, "the intention to benefit other sentient beings." It is not only a question of increasing your own happiness; you should include the happiness of others and think of alleviating their suffering. As it is said:

> Avoiding what is harmful,
> Doing what is beneficial,
> And taming your mind.
> This is the essence of Buddha's teachings.

In brief, contemplate the infallibility of karmic cause and effect by thinking, "My future is in my own hands, because what I will become or what I will experience in the future is determined by what I do right now." Think in this manner and engage in whatever is wholesome and beneficial.

The Dissatisfactory Nature of Samsara

Even if you have managed to find a precious human body, you will still be subject to the sufferings that are experienced by everyone without exception. These are the suffering of birth, old age, sickness, and death. There is also the universal suffering of being separated from a loved one, being stuck with someone you dislike, coming in contact with people you hate, and being separated from friends. Furthermore, everyone experiences difficulties in protecting what they have, either materially or in relation to others. Everyone also experiences not getting what he or she wants. There are various things we want and desire intensely, but circumstances make it impossible for us to acquire them. These sufferings are experienced by everyone without exception.

We all experience the suffering of conditioned existence, the suffering of change, and the suffering of suffering. The suffering of conditioned existence is based on indifference and is illustrated by the example of arranging a bed of hot coals. The suffering of change is based on the feeling of happiness and is illustrated by the example of sleeping on a grass mat on top of those hot coals. The suffering of suffering has the manifest feeling of suffering and is illustrated by the example of experiencing those coals blaze up when the wind blows.

The *suffering of conditioned existence* pervades all realms, from the highest of the gods to the lowest hells. Even the gods will fall to the lower realms when their karma is exhausted. This may not be seen by ordinary beings but it is clear to the *aryas* and enlightened ones. This difference in perception is comparable to having a hair on the palm of your hand and having a hair in your eye. The *Abhidharmakosha* says:

> A single hair in the palm of the hand
> Goes unnoticed but causes extreme discomfort
> If it gets into your eye.
> Immature beings are like the palm of the hand;
> They do not recognize the suffering of conditioned existence.
> And noble ones are like the eye;
> They see whatever is conditioned by suffering.

The *suffering of change* involves experiencing the sense pleasures with craving and attachment. Just as the pleasures to be had from the arrows of Mara are like licking honey from a razor blade, drinking salt water, or scratching a wound, the end of all pleasure is suffering. Since all pleasure in samsara ultimately changes into suffering, it does not transcend suffering. Even if you attain renowned states in samsara—such as that of a chakravatin or a god—this too will ultimately change to suffering. Nagarjuna's *Letter to a Friend* says:

> Even if you have become a chakravatin
> At some point you will become a servant in samsara.

The *suffering of suffering* pervades all classes of beings. The hell realms, hungry ghost realms, animal realms, human realms, demigod realms, and god realms are all subject to suffering and pain. It is said:

> Hell beings are afflicted by the fires of hell,
> Hungry ghosts are afflicted by hunger and thirst,
> Animals are afflicted by eating each other,
> Human are afflicted by not having enough,
> Gods are afflicted by recklessness,
> There is not even the tip of a needle's worth
> Of happiness in samsara.

Nagarjuna says:

> Since samsara is like that,
> There is no excellent birth anywhere among
> The gods, humans, hungry ghosts, animals, or hells;
> They are all vessels of harm.

Contemplating these aspects of samsaric suffering, which are experienced by each and every one of us regardless of position, wealth, beauty, or talent, we realize samsara is an unsatisfactory state and something that we should transcend. Generate a sense of despair from recognizing the true nature of samsara. Understand that the samsaric condition is a prison, because once you realize the imprisoning nature of samsara, you will develop an intense desire to be free of it. Once you have developed that intense desire to become free from this state, your priorities will gradually change, because you will realize there is much more to existence than pursuing this or that temporary pleasure or happiness.

Once you have a real understanding of the dissatisfactory nature of samsara, you will want to flee from it, just as animals flee in all directions when a forest catches fire. Cut through clinging and flee, the way a bird escapes from a freezing lake. Cut through attachment and flee, like a ship's captain would flee from an island of cannibals. Flee to the other shore of samsara, without corrupting your vows, just as you would preserve the raft you use to cross a river. The way to flee the samsaric condition is to accumulate the wealth of merit and wisdom. You should become rich in inner qualities and develop the richness of the mind.

You should also examine the samsaric condition and compare it to the state of nirvana to see the difference. Samsara is full of suffering and dissatisfaction and nirvana is a state of peace and contentment. When you have truly understood this, you should develop an attitude where you not only want to become free of this condition, but you want to do so to help others who are also stuck in this condition. The attainment of buddhahood is a desirable goal, not only for yourself, but because it is the only thing that will ultimately benefit others. Contemplate the dissatisfactory nature of samsara in this manner. When you can appreciate the fact that samsara is a prison you have mistaken for a home, the desire for liberation will become very intense. Therefore, think of samsara as a prison from which you want to escape at the first opportunity.

This concludes the contemplations on the four ordinary preliminaries. Now we will turn to the four extraordinary preliminaries.

The Four Extraordinary Preliminaries

The four extraordinary preliminaries consist of refuge and prostration, Vajrasattva, mandala offerings, and the practice of guru yoga. We practice refuge and prostrations to train body and mind and make them workable, we practice Vajrasattva to purify the defilements and obscurations that contaminate the mind, we practice mandala offerings to accumulate merit and wisdom, and we practice guru yoga to actualize the spiritual qualities.

Refuge and Prostrations

When we speak of refuge we should think, "What sort of person or god can give us protection?" Perhaps it would be someone with power and influence, such as Brahma or Vishnu. To grant proper protection to either humans or nonhumans, such a being must have the ability to overcome the delusions that are the cause of suffering, because unless such a being is free from delusions, he or she could not provide any protection. However, when we look at God or gods or other human beings, we see that none of them are proper objects of refuge because they are not free from delusions.

When we look at the Triple Gem—the Buddha, his teachings, and the community of followers—we realize all three of them are oriented toward the removal of suffering, the delusions that cause suffering, and the attainment of enlightenment. On the relative level, the Triple Gem is the real object of refuge, but ultimately our own buddhamind is the sole object of refuge. Only by taking refuge in the Buddha, Dharma, and Sangha for protection will we overcome all manner of fear. The *Sagaramatipariprccha sutra* says:

> There is no teacher like the Buddha,
> There is no refuge like the genuine Dharma,
> There is no group more supreme than the Sangha.

The *Nirvana sutra* says:

> Anyone who takes refuge in the Three Jewels
> Will attain fearlessness.

If we want to free ourselves from the samsaric condition and achieve liberation, we must take refuge in the Triple Gem, with an intense desire to eliminate all suffering, because there is no other real guide apart from a fully enlightened being. To attain the state of Buddha, there is no other path than the Dharma because it provides techniques for eliminating delusion. To effectively follow the path of the Buddha and his teachings, there is no other source of spiritual inspiration and encouragement than fellow practitioners pursuing the same path.

By taking refuge in the Buddha, Dharma, and Sangha, we can move very rapidly toward our destination of buddhahood. Furthermore, if we take refuge in the Buddha, Dharma, and Sangha, we will not get lost, because we will not be without guidance and will not encounter insurmountable obstacles and difficulties on the path. Taking refuge in the Triple Gem helps to clear the mind of various contaminants so we will encounter fewer obstacles and difficulties in life, and that will ultimately lead to the attainment of enlightenment. You should take refuge in the Buddha, Dharma, and Sangha with this attitude and understand the benefit of taking refuge and the harm of not taking it. The *Sutralamkara* says:

> Because it protects from all harm,
> From lower states, unskillful methods,
> From wrong views and the hinayana,
> It is known as the genuine refuge.

The Practice

In the space in front of you, visualize an immense tree with one trunk and many leafy branches and imagine it can grant all wishes. In the middle of the tree is a lotus-seat resting upon a throne adorned with many precious jewels and gems. A sun-and-moon disk are lying on top of the thrown, upon which sits your guru, who is the embodiment of all the spiritual qualities of Vajradhara, the symbol of buddhahood itself. Vajradhara is dark blue in color, with one face and two hands. He sits in a cross-legged position adorned with rich garments, anklets, and bracelets. In his left hand he holds a bell, and in his right hand he holds a vajra. His two hands are crossed at his heart center. Visualize Vajradhara as someone with exceptional beauty and radiance, with a slight smile on his face. Imagine he is very pleased and is quite awe-inspiring.

From the crown of his head up into the sky, visualize the lineage lamas of the Kagyu tradition clustered together like clouds. Various dakas and dakinis hover about in space under the lineage masters. Surrounding the base of the throne are the wrathful and peaceful protectors as the symbolic representations of the innate wakefulness of mind. Imagine these protectors are there to deal with any obstacles you may encounter during your practice. The protectors have a sense of wrathfulness in their posture, gaze, and expression.

To the right of the lineage tree, visualize the Buddha surrounded by all the buddhas of the past, present, and future. At the back of the lineage tree is the collection of teachings contained in the three baskets of the Buddhist canon. To the left of the lineage tree are all the spiritually advanced beings and bodhisattvas with bare feet and shaven heads. On the ground are varieties of sentient beings, both human and nonhuman. Include all of your enemies and friends amongst the humans; everyone who has caused harm to your person and everyone who has been a support to you. Imagine that all sentient beings are present and that no one is excluded. At this point, you should recite the refuge formula while thinking that the whole varieties of sentient beings that are present are reciting it along with you. The refuge formula starts by saying:

> I and all sentient beings as infinite as space, take refuge in the lama, who is the source from which the unequalled qualities of the body, speech, and mind of the Buddha originate. We take refuge in the mandalas of devas. We take refuge in the Buddhas. We take refuge in the Dharma. We take refuge in the Sangha. We take refuge in the glorious dakas, dakinis, and dharmapalas of wisdom.

While reciting the refuge formula, meditate on the refuge tree by focusing your mind on the objects of visualization, while maintaining awareness and concentration. The refuge formula should be followed by the generation of bodhichitta, which consists of generating the four *Brahmaviharas*. You should say:

May all sentient beings have happiness and the cause of happiness.
May all sentient beings be free from suffering and the cause of suffering.
May all sentient beings not be separated from the supreme joy that is completely devoid of suffering.
May all sentient beings remain in a state of equanimity free from craving, grasping, hatred, and resentment of those who are far and near.

At this point, start doing the prostrations as many times as you can or for the number of times you have set yourself, while imagining that all other beings are prostrating with you with joy in their hearts. When you want to conclude the practice, dissolve the visualization of the refuge tree into light. Imagine the light entering your body and your body, speech, and mind becoming inseparable from the body, speech, and mind of all the buddhas, bodhisattvas, and protectors. Remain in that state of inseparability and meditate for some time. Let your mind remain lucid, without trying to identify anything or think of anything. Simply let the mind rest. As soon as thought forms start to arise, dedicate the merit for the benefit of all sentient beings by chanting the following verse:

From the merit I have accumulated through this practice,
May I and other sentient beings attain the state of mahamudrahood
And establish all beings in that state without delay.

The Generation of Bodhichitta

Something about the generation of bodhichitta should be explained here. There are two different ways to generate bodhichitta. One is in keeping with the tradition of the hinayana and the other is in keeping with the tradition of the mahayana. The hinayana method emphasizes the importance of attaining enlightenment for your own benefit, and its aim is to attain arhathood or pratyekabuddhahood. The mahayana method emphasizes the importance of developing both method and wisdom simultaneously. If you simply rely on the method of the hinayana, you cannot attain buddhahood. You will only attain the state of an *arhat* or "foe destroyer" or a *pratyekabuddha* or "solitary realizer." It is said:

> To become a shravaka or a pratyekabuddha
> Creates a lasting hindrance to the attainment of awakening.

It is also said:

> You fall to the state of a shravaka
> If you lack compassion and wisdom.

You have to generate bodhichitta according to the mahayana method. You must first understand the nature of bodhichitta. The mahayana classifies bodhichitta as either relative bodhichitta or absolute bodhichitta. The *Samadhinirmocana sutra* says:

> There are two types of bodhichitta: relative bodhichitta and ultimate bodhichitta.

The characteristic of bodhichitta is to benefit others, which is the aspect of relative bodhichitta. This involves love and compassion for all sentient creatures. We must have humility and compassion to practice relative bodhichitta. The *Abhisamayalamkara* says:

> The characteristic of bodhichitta is

To cultivate the wish for complete enlightenment
For the welfare of others.

Bodhichitta or the "enlightened attitude" is developed gradually through different stages on the path. According to the mahayana tradition, there are ten stages we must traverse before attaining full enlightenment. The first seven are known as "sullied stages" and the last three are known as "unsullied stages." The *Abhidharmakosha* says:

The cultivation of bodhichitta on the bhumis
Involves belief, the altruistic intention, spiritual maturation
And the removal of obscurations.

The potency of the enlightened attitude is cultivated, developed, and nurtured until we realize absolute bodhichitta or absolute "enlightened mind." Relative bodhichitta should be cultivated in two stages. As the *Bodhicharyavatara* says:

Bodhichitta or the enlightened attitude
Should be cultivated in two stages:
The first is intention and the second is action.

The difference between these two stages is that even if you are incapable of doing anything for others, you can begin by developing an attitude that wishes to benefit them. The *Bodhicharyavatara* says again:

The difference between the two bodhichittas
Is like wanting to take a journey
And actually being on a journey.

The object of bodhichitta is ordinary sentient beings that are as infinite as space. You should therefore think, "Until the delusions of sentient beings are brought to an end, I will work towards achieving enlightenment."

The development of relative bodhichitta comes from developing concern for the welfare of others, and through it we come to realize the true nature of mind, which is absolute bodhichitta. In other words, through cultivating the relative enlightened attitude, we realize the absolute enlightened mind.

Absolute bodhichitta refers to the innate nature of mind, which is empty yet luminous and not polluted by defilements and obscurations. There are two types of defilements or obscurations: emotional conflicts and conceptual distortions. The intrinsic and immaculate nature of mind is absolute bodhichitta. The *Samadhinirmocana sutra* says:

> Absolute bodhichitta is beyond the empirical consciousness, devoid of all empirical characteristics, luminous and inseparable from absolute truth. This unwavering, luminous mind—which is like a flame on a windless night—is absolute bodhichitta.

Even though absolute bodhichitta is present within our minds, we do not recognize its presence until we reach the first stage of the bodhisattva path. This understanding gradually grows until the tenth stage.

To recognize our own innate nature of mind or absolute bodhichitta, it is essential to generate relative bodhichitta. This essentially involves generating concern for other sentient beings, both human and nonhuman, and working for their benefit. To generate relative bodhichitta, we must first take the bodhisattva vow from a teacher. Asanga's *Bodhisattvabhumi* says:

> It is completely permissible to use a buddha image to

> take the bodhisattva vow; it is not essential to have a living teacher present.

If you are not in possession of a statue, you could use a painting or any other image. You could even simply visualize a buddha in front of you and recite the bodhisattva formula to that. The *Shikshasamuchaya* says:

> Imagine all the buddhas and bodhisattvas of past, present, and future are in the sky before you and then take the vow in their presence.

The way in which the bodhisattva vow is taken varies from tradition to tradition, but the most popular method, which is the one we are using here, originates from Nagarjuna and Shantideva.

When you are ready to take the bodhisattva vow, place the buddha statue on a platform and put all kinds of offerings before it. It is important to make these offerings because they will generate merit. Once that is done, you should kneel in front of the shrine, facing the Buddha statue, and recite the Seven Limb Prayer three times as follows:

> I prostrate to the Buddha of the three times and
> make offerings to you.
> I offer flowers, incense, light, perfume, and many
> other things, both in substance and in my
> imagination.
> I confess all my transgressions and take delight
> in your teachings.
> Please turn the wheel of the Dharma and
> continue to expound the teachings.
> I rejoice in the merit of all the buddhas,
> bodhisattvas, and protectors.
> I ask you not to pass into nirvana but to look after
> all sentient beings.

Whatever merit I may have accumulated,
I dedicate to all sentient beings, so they may attain enlightenment.

Once the Seven Limb Prayer has been recited, take refuge in the Triple Gem. Visualize the Buddha sitting on a throne flanked by four lions. The Buddha is golden in color, with his left hand resting in his lap and his right hand resting on his right knee. He is sitting in a cross-legged position and surrounded by all the bodhisattvas. Think of the Buddha as the guide, his teachings as the path, and the spiritual community as your companions on the path. Then think, "I take the bodhisattva vow in the same manner as the Buddhas and bodhisattvas of the past took this commitment. I take this vow with the sole purpose of alleviating the suffering of other sentient beings."

At this point, read out the following section of the *Bodhicharyavatara* three times while imagining you have now fully taken the bodhisattva vow:

Just as previous buddhas have generated compassion,
I too wish to train in the practice of the bodhisattvas.
Just as previous buddhas engaged in this in a systematic way
In order to benefit other sentient beings,
I too, will give birth to bodhichitta and follow the practice of the bodhisattvas.
From now on, until attaining enlightenment
I will preserve this compassionate mind
By thinking of this precious human body, which I now possess.
I have now joined the family of the Buddhas.
From now onwards, whatever I do,
I will ensure it is in accordance with the bodhisattva practice,

So that the tradition will not be stained by my
defilements.

Then chant the following verse:

Due to my good fortune,
Today I have become part of the family of the
Buddha.
From now on, in keeping with the family of the
Buddha,
I will continue to work for the benefit of beings,
So the purity of the family will not be polluted.

Then rest in a feeling of great joy and rejoice, feeling all sentient beings are witnessing this. The consequence of taking this vow is that you will not abandon sentient beings, no matter what happens. That is the essence of the commitment. You should also avoid doing harm and actively engage in doing what is beneficial.

As stated earlier, relative bodhichitta has two aspects: the intention to benefit others and actively engaging in activities that alleviate the suffering of others. As for the first, you must think of the suffering of sentient beings and then think about the benefit that comes from thinking such thoughts. You should also try to generate merit and wisdom. The second aspect of relative bodhichitta is accomplished in the six *paramitas* or six "perfections." These consist of the practices of generosity, moral conduct, patience, exertion, meditation, and the cultivation of wisdom. By practicing the six paramitas, you will be able to alleviate the suffering of others, so the benefit of generating bodhichitta is immense. The *Shridattagrihaptiparipricha sutra* says:

If the merit accumulated
Through the practice of bodhichitta

> Could be transformed into a substance,
> It would fill the whole of space.

The *Bodhicharyavatara* says:

> The only way to escape the prison of samsara
> Is to generate bodhichitta.
> You will then travel to the state of enlightenment
> with ease
> And become worthy of respect
> From both humans and nonhumans.
>
> Furthermore, if you have taken the bodhisattva vow,
> It will leave such positive impressions in your mind
> stream
> That merit will be generated continuously, without
> cessation,
> Even while you are asleep or distracted by your
> senses.

Just as the merit of the bodhisattva vow is immense, the harm incurred by abandoning it is also immense. There is no greater obstacle to your spiritual path than abandoning the bodhisattva vow. If you take this vow and then subsequently abandon your commitment, you will have deceived all sentient beings. It is therefore of immense importance that you examine both the benefits and harm involved in taking this particular commitment and then commit yourself to the practice with proper understanding. You will ensure your future enlightenment by taking this bodhisattva vow. This is how one should think of bodhichitta practice.

Vajrasattva

The function of Vajrasattva practice is to purify your

defilements and obscurations. Generally speaking, whether you experience positive or negative karma, they are both produced by delusions in the mind. Nagarjuna's *Precious Garland* says:

> Every action is preceded by a mental act.
> For this reason, mind is most important.

Vasubhandhu's *Abhidharmakosha* says:

> Intention is a mental act
> Which brings about verbal and physical behavior.

A deluded or afflicted mind that is polluted by grasping, clinging, hatred, and so on gives rise to the various unwholesome thoughts and actions. These may be actions directly committed by ourselves, atrocious deeds that we have encouraged others to commit, or the wholesome deeds of others that we have taken delight in. Furthermore, even if we attempt to engage in religious activities like worship and prayer, they will still only produce negative results if they are imbued with delusions sustained by grasping, clinging, hatred and so on.

There are two types of obscurations: obscurations of emotional conflicts and obscurations of conceptual distortion. The first obscuration hinders our attaining liberation from the samsaric condition. The second obscuration hinders the attainment of enlightenment. In Buddhist psychology, the obscuration of emotional conflicts is listed in many different ways. Briefly stated, the six primary emotions of grasping, hatred, pride, jealousy, ignorance, and two-mindedness (extreme skepticism that hinders our ability to commit to anything), can be reduced to just three: grasping, hatred, and ignorance. The obscuration of conceptual distortion refers to the dualism of our conceptual categories. To put it simply, we have an innate tendency to view things as inherently existing.

Negative actions will be purified if they are confessed. A confession must incorporate the four powers. These are: 1) the power of regret, 2) the power of antidote, 3) the power of support, and 4) the power of commitment.

The Power of Regret

Vajrasattva practice is how we purify our mind of its defilements, obscurations, and negative karma. The most expedient way of purifying the mind of negative karma is to feel regret. The most important aspect of regret is the ability to verbalize what the regrettable things we have done and bring them out into the open. This is known as the power of regret. The power of regret is implemented by thinking, "I have done many terrible things in the past, either by fighting my enemies or trying to protect myself and my friends. Upon reflection, I realize this has done nothing but cause more harm to my self and others. The relatives, friends, and loved ones for whom I did these misdeeds will not be able to accompany me at the time of death. They will be left behind and I will have to carry the negative karma I have accumulated into the postmortem state alone."

Then think, "I should not waste my energy by putting myself in the difficult situation of fighting off enemies or currying favor with friends and relatives, because ultimately, it does not benefit either myself or those associated with me." The *Shridattagrihaptiparipricha sutra* says:

> When the time of death comes,
> Your parents, brothers, sisters, children,
> Wife, husband, servants,
> Material possessions, and physical prowess
> Will be left behind.

> However, the negative karma you have created
> Will follow you relentlessly.

You should therefore think, "If I have not been able to purify my mind of negative karma, that karma will follow me into the next life and cause further suffering and distress."

Having realized the importance of purifying your mind of negative karma, you should now employ a method for doing so, because if your mind is not purified of defilements and the negative karma that arises from them, you will die without ever dealing with them. Shantideva's *Bodhicharyavatara* says:

> Do not waste time while you are alive
> You may die at any moment, without purifying your mind.
> Engage in the practice of purification
> And free your mind from its obscurations and negativities.

The *Bodhicharyavatara* also says:

> Death is untrustworthy; we never know when it will come.
> It does not discriminate between things that are done or half-done
> Or things that have not yet begun.
> It does not discriminate between sick and healthy;
> It strikes anyone.

The Power of the Antidote

When you begin to reflect on your actions, you may be overwhelmed by the number of misdeeds you have committed and become discouraged. You should not feel this way, because no matter how much negative karma you have created, there is none that cannot be destroyed by creating wholesome karma. The *Nirvana sutra* says:

> Even doing one good deed can rectify many unwholesome deeds.

The *Suvarnaprabhasottama sutra* says:

> You may have created negative karma for an infinite number of lives,
> But if you can muster up the courage to confess those deeds
> And bring them out into the open,
> All that negative karma will be purified in that moment.

It is just like washing dirty laundry. There is no spot on a piece of cloth that cannot be washed out and there is no negative karma that cannot be purified.

The Power of Commitment

This power relates to the commitment not to repeat your mistakes. Once you notice the misdeeds you have performed in the past, acknowledge them, verbalize them, and bring them out into the open: you have been purged of these pollutions. The next step is to make a commitment not to repeat those same mistakes. This commitment will ensure your mistake is not repeated over and over. It is not enough to identify, acknowledge, verbalize, and bring them out into the open, you must also make a commitment to not repeat the same mistakes. You should make the supplication:

> Guides, please hear me:

I acknowledge all of my negative deeds and
thoughts;
Since they are not positive
I shall not repeat them.

The Power of Support

This refers to reliance on the Triple Gem and the cultivation of bodhichitta. Through relying on the Triple Gem and cultivating bodhichitta, we can sustain ourselves in practices that will combat our inveterate tendency to indulge in unwholesome actions. We may not have the strength to deal with negative karmic tendencies by ourselves, but if we can draw on the strength of the Triple Gem, the power of compassion, and the wisdom of relative and absolute bodhichitta, we will sustain our practice and be less likely to fall victim to our inveterate tendencies and karmic traces and dispositions. The *Bodhicharyavatara* says:

Although you may have done overwhelming
negative acts
Reliance on this will bring immediate liberation,
Just like relying on a warrior when greatly afraid.
Why do those who are heedful not rely on this?

The sutras have told many different stories to illustrate the efficacy of these four powers. For example, there is the story of Angulimala who murdered 999 human beings. When he subsequently came into contact with the Buddha and worked through his negative karma, he did not have to experience any of the consequences of his actions. There are also stories of people who have murdered their parents, yet through subsequent reflection on the four powers, were delivered from the samsaric condition and attained many spiritual qualities. Negative karmas are created by a disturbed mind devoid of mindfulness and awareness.

When that same mind becomes mindful and aware, all the obscurations and defilements are dispersed.

The Method of Vajrasattva Practice

You may wonder at this point, "If the four powers are important for mental purification, which power relates to the practice of Vajrasattva?" Vajrasattva practice is related to one of the supreme methods—the power of the antidote. To practice Vajrasattva, do the following visualization:

Sit in a cross-legged position and visualize a white lotus resting on a moon disk upon the crown of your head. On the moon disk is a five-pronged white vajra, marked in its middle with the syllable HUM. Light radiates from that HUM and spreads in the ten directions. It makes offerings to all the buddhas and bodhisattvas and then gathers back into the five-pronged vajra, at which point the vajra is transformed into Vajrasattva; the embodiment of the nature of your mind and your guru.

Vajrasattva is white in color to symbolize the purity of being uncorrupted by the defilements and obscurations. He has one face and two hands and sits in a cross-legged position. In his right hand is a five-pronged vajra, which is held against his heart. In his left hand is a bell, which is resting on his left hip. He is adorned with many precious garments and his hair is tied in a topknot, the tip of which is adorned with precious gems. He is wearing many precious anklets, bracelets, and so on. He should be visualized as endowed with exceptional beauty and translucent radiance. He manifests as an insubstantial appearance so that he appears just like a reflection of the moon in water or like objects reflected in a mirror.

In his heart chakra is a lunar disk in the middle of which is a white HUM, with his mantra OM VAJRASATTVA HUM revolving around it. Each syllable is so white and brilliant that it is like a garland of moving pearls radiating light.

The light attracts the lamas, buddhas, bodhisattvas, and protectors and makes offerings to them, so that they all become very pleased and satisfied. Then, one by one, these innumerable buddhas and bodhisattvas gradually dissolve into Vajrasattva so that he is inseparable from them. At that point, say the following supplication:

> Oh, Vajrasattva, please purify all the defilements, obscurations, and negative karma that I and all sentient beings have created in this and previous lives.

Imagine Vajrasattva responds to this plea while visualizing his mantra producing white nectar that slowly fills his body and then starts to drip from the toe of the right foot onto the crown of your head. Imagine all the negativities that you have created from beginningless time as well as any sickness or mental distress you may have being transformed into blood, pus, and bile. The nectar that is flowing from Vajrasattva's heart center into your body through the crown of your head gradually pushes this vile fluid out through the openings of your body. Then visualize that your body is completely purified, translucent, energetic, and healthy. It is so filled with nectar so that it overflows back out through the crown of your head and touches Vajrasattva's foot. Concentrate on that and recite the hundred-syllable mantra of Vajrasattva for as long as you feel comfortable. When you wish to conclude the practice, fold your hands together and say the following prayer:

> Oh, Victorious One, I have committed many transgressions due to my ignorance and lack of understanding. Please, Vajrasattva, grant me your protection, for you are full of compassion and love. I take refuge in you as the protector of all sentient beings.

Then say the following confession:

> I confess all the negative karma I have created through body, speech, and mind and bring it out into the open. Please grant me strength and bless me so that my defilements and obscurations are purified and cleansed.

Imagine Vajrasattva smiling with joy in response to this confession. He then says the following words:

> Oh, son or daughter of noble family, your defilements and obscurations have now been purified from this day forth.

Vajrasattva dissolves into light and is absorbed through the crown of your head. Imagine that the body, speech, and mind of Vajrasattva and your own body, speech, and mind become completely identical and inseparable and then remain in a state of meditation until a thought arises in your mind. Then dedicate the merit by saying:

> May I quickly become Vajrasattva
> And lead every sentient being
> To their enlightened state
> Due to these merits.

If you do this practice properly, you may detect signs of progress. For example, your body may feel light and you may need less sleep and feel resilient and awake. You may have a general sense of well-being. You may dream of taking a bath, running around naked, or flying through space. You may dream that your body is emitting blood and pus. You may dream of wearing white garments or drinking milk or yogurt. All of these things are regarded as a sign of progress. However, these kinds of dreams do not mean you should stop the practice. You should continue the practice until the whole course is completed.

Mandala Offering

The practice of offering mandalas is geared toward the accumulation of merit and wisdom. If you engage in the six paramitas of generosity, morality, patience, exertion, concentration, and discriminating awareness with a pure motivation, you will accumulate merit and wisdom automatically. According to Chandrakirti's *Madhyamakavatara*, the first three paramitas of generosity, morality, and patience increase merit while exertion, concentration, and discriminating awareness increase wisdom. However, according to Asanga's *Bodhisattvabhumi*, generosity and morality increase merit, discriminating awareness increases wisdom, while patience, exertion, and concentration increase both merit and wisdom. Others have said that generosity increases merit, while the last five increase wisdom.

The accumulation of merit and wisdom must be practiced simultaneously. In the context of mandala offering, you should realize the best form of creating merit and wisdom is to make offerings to enlightened beings. As you have the intention of attaining buddhahood yourself, you should regard the buddhas and bodhisattvas as examples. You emulate them and make offerings to them as a form of service, because this service will increase your merit and wisdom and will propel you to the state of buddhahood. The *Abhisamayalamkara* says:

> When you arise from making offerings to the buddha
> And gathering the accumulation of wisdom and merit,
> The wisdom that does not conceptualize the ultimate
> Is said to be superior.

Mandala Practice

As for the actual mandala offering itself, there are many different systems, but they all come down to two: the *mandala of practice* and the *mandala of offering*. If you possess two mandala disks, the disk of better quality should be used for the practice mandala and the one of lesser quality for the offering mandala. If you only have one mandala disk, you can use it for both purposes. If you do not have even one disk, you can visualize a disk instead. The mandala itself should be circular in shape and rise slightly in the middle. Its top should be shiny, slippery, and free from any faults or cracks, and you should make sure it does not become scratched.

Polish the practice mandala three times on a clockwise, circular motion with scented water or ointment, using your right hand. Then repeat this motion with a handful of rice or other grain. Place a small portion of rice in the middle and at the specified points on the mandala, using mindfulness to ensure they do not fluctuate in size. The first pile of rice should be placed in the middle and the others should be placed in the four directions. Then visualize all the buddhas, bodhisattvas, and gurus of the Kagyu lineage are present along with all the divinities. Place the practice mandala on the altar while visualizing that the lineage lamas, buddhas, and bodhisattvas are hovering in space before you.

Pick up the offering mandala and hold it in your left hand while grasping rice in your right hand. While reciting Vajrasattva's hundred-syllable mantra once, clean the mandala disk as you did before in a clockwise direction. Imagine the mandala disk is completely cleansed while simultaneously imagining your own defilements and obscurations are being cleared away. Practice complete concentration and mindfulness at all times so that there is synchronization between the recitations of the purification mantra, the visualization, your thoughts about your own purified defilements and obscurations, and the physical act of placing the piles of rice on the disk. Utter the mantra OM VAJRA BHUMI AH HUM followed by the usual mandala offering formula:

> The ground is sprinkled with scented water and scattered flowers in the four directions. I offer you Mount Meru and the four continents adorned with the sun and the moon with the intention of attaining buddhahood. May all sentient beings enter into Buddha's pure realm.

Conclude with the following verse:

> All the gurus who have actualized the potential of their body, speech, and mind, please accept this offering of mine, which symbolizes the outer, inner, and secret offerings. After accepting my body, material possessions, and this physical world, please grant me the realization of absolute truth. Please grant me your blessing so that I realize mahamudrahood.

The outer offering is the actual mandala disk, the inner offering is the visualization, and the secret offering is the realization of the innate nature of mind and the nonduality of the object (the offering) and the subject (the one making the offering). If you wish, you can also recite the Seven Limb Prayer. When the session is nearing its end, imagine all the buddhas, bodhisattvas, and lamas who came to witness this now dissolve into you and become inseparable from you. At that point, dedicate the merit for the benefit of all sentient beings:

> Through the merit I have created through this
> practice,

May the omniscient ones grant me the courage
To defeat the forces of defiling tendencies.
May sentient beings who are tossed about
By the waves of birth, old age, sickness, and death
Be delivered from the ocean of samsara.

While doing this practice, you may have certain signs of progress, such as not having to eat too much or finding that teachings that did not previously make sense now become intelligible. Things that you have forgotten may be recalled with precision, you may have a sense of well-being, be able to direct your mind to various purposes, and dream of women who present you with food and drink. You may also dream of going uphill, going into gardens and picking flowers, going somewhere in new clothes, wearing jewelry, swimming across rivers, building a bridge, or traveling somewhere in a ship. You may dream of looking into or polishing a mirror, blowing trumpets, beating a drum, playing musical instruments, or admiring frescoes in a temple or monastery. It is not sufficient to have only one dream; these dreams have to be recurring to be regarded as an indication of success with the practice.

Guru Yoga

The function of guru yoga is to rapidly ripen your spiritual qualities. This practice is the root of your meditative experience and authentic understanding. It involves the meeting of a student with the relevant attributes and a teacher with the appropriate qualities. If this meeting occurs, it will be very easy for you to attain mahamudrahood in one lifetime. This is particularly so in relation to the Kagyu tradition, which is why our tradition is called the "practice lineage" or "lineage of experience." Since the emphasis is on practice and immediate experience, the interaction between student and teacher is of utmost importance. It is important for both teacher and student to discern whether there is any connection between them, because in many cases, it is a question of reawakening your karmic link and rapport with each other.

The Qualities of a Teacher

The teacher may appear in different forms, either as a celibate, fully ordained teacher of the hinayana and mahayana teachings or the teacher may appear in the form of a tantrika who may not be celibate. The teacher must also be a master of the Four Dharmas of Gampopa—turning the mind to the dharma, making success on the path, clarifying confusion, and revealing confusion as wisdom—and he must be able to deal with these Four Dharmas in relation to the student. The teacher must also have immense compassion and patience, offer a pure mind without any ulterior motivation, be eloquent in presenting the teachings, and have learning and great understanding. The teacher should be not be someone who is excessively concerned with worldly matters but be an example of a spiritual person. The teacher must also be skilful in answering questions and give answers appropriate to each student's needs.

If the teacher is a fully ordained monk, he must be someone who observes the vinaya rules so students can see him as an embodiment of the vinaya and be inspired. Such a monk must also possess the three qualities of a scholar: exposition, reasoning ability, and the ability to compose texts. In other words, he must have the ability to expound the teachings, he must be able to present the teachings by offering good reasons, and he must be skilled in writing. Such a monk will instill the qualities of the "three trainings" in students: the training in moral discipline, the training in meditation, and the training in wisdom.

If the teacher is not only a monk but also a teacher of the mahayana, he or she must possess certain additional qualities. For example, he must be well versed in the mahayana traditions and practice bodhichitta to such a degree that he would never abandon the bodhisattva vow, even at risk of losing his life. The *Madhyamakalankara* says:

> The mahayana teacher must be peaceful in
> demeanor,
> Learned, with proper understanding
> And skill in the art of teaching.
> He must have great love, compassion,
> Concern for others,
> And have abandoned worries and a disturbed mind.

Other qualities listed as necessary for a mahayana teacher are gentleness with others, being without pride, not being given to despair, a lucid mind, learning in many different fields, good understanding, and not being immersed in temporal and immediate concerns. The master Chandrakirti states:

> A proper teacher is able to assess the needs of the
> student,
> To understand the mind of the student,
> And to teach in accordance with the temperament of
> the student.
> It is a wise teacher who is able to attract students.
> A fool will never become a teacher.

A tantric master has realized the nature of the deities to be essentially the same as their own mind and therefore is a yogi and master of tantric practices. The *Kalachakra tantra* says:

> A vajra master must be someone who has not transgressed any of the samaya vows of the vajrayana

> tradition, has purified the defilements, and realized the nature of mind to be the same as the nature of Vajrasattva.

However, in this day and age, most teachers have some good and some bad qualities. It is almost impossible to find someone who has no fault whatsoever, so it is a matter of trying to discern who has a greater number of positive qualities and then following that teacher. These criteria should be a guideline rather an injunction to find someone with no faults whatsoever. Even if you cannot find a teacher who meets these descriptions, at the very least rely on someone who is unselfish, who is able to abide by the precepts of the three yanas and to lead students on the path of spirituality rather than dragging them down. The teacher should not have the same conflicting emotions as the student, in terms of wanting to protect friends and destroy enemies. Those are the essential qualities of a teacher.

The Qualities of a Student

Many different qualities are also listed for students, but the basic one is to make your commitment complete and not half-hearted once you have made your choice and accepted someone as your teacher. You should have real and genuine trust in that teacher and real confidence in his or her abilities. The student must have recognized the dissatisfactory nature of samsara and experienced a sense of urgency about wanting to escape from it. At the same time, he or she must have compassion and the desire to alleviate the suffering of others. The student must also make the commitment to achieve enlightenment in this very body and lifetime.

If students follow a particular teacher because they stand to get a free meal or because they will attract the attention of others by associating with that teacher, this would be no different than hanging around with somebody famous and does not constitute a proper relationship between teacher and student. For this reason, it is important for both the teacher and the student to have rapport. The teacher must have the appropriate qualities and attributes, and the student must have the requisite qualities to become a proper vessel for the teachings. The student must show humility and respect to the teacher, because without humility, it will be impossible to appreciate and receive the teachings properly. Gampopa says:

> To realize mahamudrahood,
> You must rely on certain methods and instructions.
> These methods and instructions come from
> a teacher.
> To get the most benefit from them,
> You must have humility toward your teacher.

The *Mahayanuttaratantra* says:

> Through humility, you realize absolute truth.
> The sun is radiant at all times,
> But the blind never see that radiance.
> In the same way, without humility,
> You will never be able to recognize absolute truth.

Humility must therefore precede your spiritual quest. Lorepa says:

> You should first develop conditioned humility.
> This will gradually develop into unconditioned
> humility,
> Which in turn will awaken the recognition
> That the nature of the teacher's mind
> And the nature of your own mind are inseparable.

The *Kalachakra tantra* says:

> Even if you engage in the most sublime activities
> For three countless eons—
> Making offerings to religious objects or saving the lives of animals—
> It will not help you realize buddhahood in this lifetime.
> However, if you establish a proper relationship with your teacher,
> It is possible to attain buddhahood in this very body.

The sutras say:

> Humility is the antidote to the demon of egocentricity
> Because it awakens the gate of liberation.
> Humility germinates the seeds of your spiritual qualities
> And the trunk of enlightenment will grow from them.

You should thereby realize the significance of humility and inclination. Then, armed with these two attributes, you should engage in the practice of guru yoga, because the benefits of doing so are immense. The *Sanchayagathaprajnaparamita sutra* says:

> Good students approach the teacher with a sense of humility
> Because they know that relying on a skilful teacher,
> Will make them just as realized and skilled as that teacher.

The same sutra says:

> It is difficult to cross to the other shore

Without a boat.
In the same way, no matter how learned or skilled
  you are,
You will not be able to cross the ocean of samsara,
Without an appropriate connection with a teacher.

The *Dam tshig bkod pa* says:

You may visualize numerous deities
And engage in that meditation indefinitely,
But that approach is far surpassed
By the benefit of practicing guru yoga.

The *Pancakrama* says:

If someone slips and rolls down a cliff,
You will not be able to arrest their fall
No matter how hard you try to stop their momentum.
In the same way, if you make a proper connection
  with a teacher,
You will not be able to resist attaining liberation
  even if you try.

Naropa says:

The practice of guru yoga
Unlocks the treasury of all spiritual qualities.

The *Ati bkod pa* says:

If you visualize the guru on the crown of your head,
The benefits will be immense.

Gotsangpa says:

There are many different kinds of deity yoga,

> Involving many different types of visualization,
> But the practice of guru yoga
> Produces more benefit than any of them.

Sakya Pandita says:

> The benefit of practicing guru yoga is incomparable.
> No other practice can generate so much benefit.

The *Pal jung gyi rnam thar* says:

> If you establish the proper reliance on the teacher, you will not be born in undesirable states. If you establish the proper reliance on the teacher, you will not fall under the influence of negative companions or regress from the mahayana path. To establish the proper reliance on the teacher means you have already gone a long distance from the state of ordinary people.

The Practice

All of these statements and quotations make clear the importance of guru yoga. You should engage in this practice to benefit other sentient beings, and with that motivation in mind, visualize your guru in the form of Vajradhara on top of your head. In essence, Vajradhara is your own guru. He is sitting on a sun-and-moon disk on a throne flanked by lions in the four directions. Vajradhara has one face and two hands. He is blue in color, which symbolizes the nature of all things. He is sitting cross-legged, holding a vajra in his right hand, a bell in his left, with his wrists crossed at the heart center. He is radiant and awe-inspiring and appears very pleased, with a half-smile on his face. He is adorned with precious garments and jewelry and his appearance is transparent and insubstantial.

All the lineage masters of the Kagyu tradition are organized around the top of Vajradhara's head. Visualize Vajradhara surrounded by buddhas, bodhisattvas, dakas, dakinis, protectors, and so on. At this point, chant the Seven Limb Prayer and then recite the following verses three times:

> Residing in the palatial mansion of the absolute truth is the glorious guru, the embodiment of the buddhas of the three times. You have the ability to actualize the nature of my mind to be the same as that of the Buddha, therefore I prostrate to you. I offering whatever possessions I have, and whatever possession I do not have, I offer in my imagination. I confess all the transgressions and misdeeds of the past and make the commitment not to repeat them in the future.
>
> May all sentient beings develop the inclination toward wholesome thoughts and deeds. May all sentient beings attain enlightenment. I beseech the guru to remain in the world and not pass into nirvana. I beseech you to continue to turn the wheel of the dharma. May I develop impartial love and compassion. May I develop the wisdom that realizes absolute truth. May I realize all that the buddhas and bodhisattvas of the past have realized. May I realize my own ordinary body as the nirmanakaya. May I realize my speech as the sambhogakaya. May I realize my own mind as the dharmakaya. May the three kayas be revealed as integrated and inseparable.

Follow this recitation with mandala offerings, in the same manner as before, and then chant the following verses:

> Guru, oh guru, please grant me the strength to overcome my self-centeredness. May I realize

> nondissatisfaction. May I realize the nature of my mind to be unborn. May my delusions be self-liberated. May I realize this very world to be the manifestation of the nature of mind.

The lineage lamas then begin to dissolve into light, which is absorbed into Vajradhara. At that point, Vajradhara becomes the embodiment of all the infinite qualities of enlightened beings. Then make the following request:

> Guru, oh guru, please grant me the four empowerments.

Visualize white light emanating from the crown of Vajradhara's head and being absorbed into your own forehead. Imagine that all the physical defilements and negative karmas you have created through misuse of your body have become purified by this light and you are empowered to do the creative imagination practices of tantra. Imagine that this has left seeds for the attainment of the *nirmanakaya*, "the physical aspect of a buddha's being."

Visualize red light emanating from the throat center of Vajradhara and being absorbed into your own throat center. Imagine that all the defilements and negative karmas you have created through misuse of your speech have become purified by this light and you are empowered to practice the yogic exercises of tantra. Imagine that this has left seeds for the attainment of the *sambhogakaya*, "the communicative aspect of a buddha's being."

Visualize blue light emanating from the heart center of Vajradhara and being absorbed into your own heart center. Imagine that all the mental defilements and negative karmas you have created through misuse of your thoughts have become purified by this light and you are empowered to transmute sexual bliss into the spiritual bliss of the tantric tradition. Imagine that this has left seeds for the actualization of the *dharmakaya*, "the authentic aspect of a buddha's being."

Then imagine that all three lights are emitted from all three centers of Vajradhara and strike the corresponding centers of your own body simultaneously in a rainbow of white, red, and blue light. This purifies all the defilements of your body, speech, and mind simultaneously, and you are empowered to practice the mahamudra that reveals awareness and emptiness as inseparable. Imagine that this has left seeds for the actualization of the *svabhavivakaya*, "the integrated aspect of a buddha's being."

Try to remain in a state of meditation without thinking about or visualizing anything. Simply remain in a state of meditation for as long as you can and then chant the following:

> The glorious and precious lama resides on a lotus in my heart chakra in the condition of inseparability from myself. Nonetheless, I ask for the blessings of your body, speech, and mind.

Imagine that Vajradhara then dissolves into light and enters your body through your crown center so that the body, speech, and mind of Vajradhara and your own body, speech, and mind become inseparable. Meditate on mahamudra for as long as you can in this way and then dedicate the merit for the benefit of all sentient beings with the following verse:

> May I quickly become you, great lama,
> And lead every sentient being
> To their enlightened state,
> Due to these merits.

You should think that this practice of guru yoga actually purifies the obscurations of your emotional conflicts and your conceptual confusion, while you simultaneously accumulate both merit and wisdom. You are thus creating the necessary conditions for realizing the three *kayas* or three "aspects of a buddha's being." Practice guru yoga with a sense of enthusiasm and delight because you are doing all these things at the same time.

An indication of success with this practice is the development of feelings of inseparability from your teacher. The thought of your teacher will frequently enter into your mind. You may have dreams in which you meet the teacher, dreams where you listen to teachings, dreams where you receive empowerments, and dreams where you manifest various lights in the form of rainbows and so on.

You should realize the importance of the four extraordinary preliminaries, because without these practices, it will be impossible to have either meditative experiences or realizations. Even though they are called "preliminary" practices, you should not understand them to be insignificant or something to complete as quickly as possible. They are the most important practice. If you do not fully integrate these ngondro practices, it would create more harm than good to go straight to the other practices. This is why you should not hurry through the four preliminaries, but take your time and do them properly. Only when you have these practices behind you can you proceed to the other practices.

The Four Conditions

To fully integrate the preliminary practices, you must take four conditions into consideration. The four conditions are 1) the causal condition, 2) the empowering condition, 3) the object condition, and 4) the proximate condition.

Causal Condition

The causal condition is the development of nonattachment, which is to no longer be dependent on external situations and material conditions. You should clearly recognize that this human body cannot be taken for granted; it has been acquired with enormous difficulty and should not be wasted. You should clearly understand the body to be transient, impermanent, and as fragile as dewdrops on the grass, and have the clear realization that while the time of death may be uncertain, it is certain that death will occur. When death arrives, nothing will be of any use except the spiritual insights you developed while alive. You must also realize that if your whole purpose in life is to pursue wealth, to protect friends and relatives, and to destroy enemies, you will not be spending your time well and are actually causing a lot of harm.

With these realizations, develop a sense of urgency, reorient your life, and learn to see things differently. First of all, it is very useful to spend time by yourself and practice, so that you have less chance of becoming seduced by the distractions of life. As long as the mind grasps after this or that, and clings to it, the result will only be distraction. It is very difficult to learn to concentrate the mind in a distracted state. For this reason, it is useful to spend time away from daily worries and engagements, at the beginning of your practice.

Empowering Condition

The empowering condition, which also needs be present for the four preliminaries to work, is to have a qualified teacher. To practice and to realize mahamudra, it is important to have a teacher who is qualified to teach mahamudra methods and give instructions on how to attain mahamudra. There are four kinds of teachers: 1) the physical teacher, 2) the teachings, 3) the symbolic teacher, and 4) the absolute truth.

The Physical Teacher

Your human teacher must possess the transmissions that have been passed down in succession from master to student, because all the necessary instructions are handed down from one generation to the next. Such a teacher must also be someone who can actually produce positive results in the practice of their student. They need the skill to convey their own understanding and realization to the student so that the student's innate intellect can be awakened. They must be skilled in using concepts and thoughts to awaken innate wisdom rather than allowing thoughts and concepts to limit the mind's potential. They also need skill in transforming negative situations and circumstances into positive ones by instigating a change of attitude.

The Teachings

It is important to find a teacher who does not discard thoughts and concepts as the cause of delusion and hanker after wisdom as something different. He or she must have realized that the nature of thoughts and concepts, when recognized for what they are, is the same as innate wisdom. That is the type of teacher you should seek if you wish to follow the mahamudra path. Furthermore, it is important to seek a teacher who can look at the various Buddhist schools as forming a whole, rather than saying that one point of view is better than another or that one tradition is superior to another. The teacher should not promote and propagate biases and dogmatism or become extremely obsessed with the words and forget about experience. If a teacher is concerned with distinguishing true from false teachings, they end up indulging in all kinds of argumentation. These things should be discarded.

The Symbolic Teacher

The symbolic teacher is the phenomenal world itself. The earth element represents the importance of having unshakeable humility as the basis for developing all good qualities, just as the earth is the basis for all the other elements to function. The water element represents the moisturizing effect of compassion, which loosens the hardened nature of human beings, just as water softens soil. The fire element represents the intellect, because it consumes conceptual confusion and illuminates the darkness of ignorance, just as fire consumes wood and fiber. The wind element represents meditative experiences and realizations, because they dismantle all false beliefs and mistaken notions, just as wind scatters things around. Space represents the reality of the phenomenal world, because emptiness is found in everything, just as space is all-encompassing.

The Absolute Truth

The absolute truth is synonymous with the nature of mind, because when you realize the nature of your own mind to be the same as the nature of an enlightened being's mind, this is also the teacher.

Among these different forms of teacher, the physical teacher is the most important, because without a physical teacher, you will not be able to appreciate the significance of the other teachers. Only through the instructions and guidance of a physical teacher will you understand the importance of relating to these other forms of guru.

Object Condition

The object condition is about having the right object of intention. This condition relates to the different schools, traditions, lineages, philosophical systems, and tantric traditions of Buddhism. This includes the Madhyamaka and Yogacara schools of mahayana thought, and the anuyoga and anuttarayoga tantras of the vajrayana. You should regard the mahamudra system as all-encompassing, instead of trying to determine which school has the right view and which tradition has the best method. Otherwise, you will only end up reinforcing your own presuppositions and biases, and ultimately obscure reality and hinder your own realization. Understand that mahamudra contains all these schools and traditions, instead of trying to establish the mahamudra view as separate from them. Mahamudra deals with reality as it is. Reality cannot be limited by saying that it favors this view as opposed to that view. Mahamudra is the name given to reality-as-such, and reality-as-such is devoid of all empirical determinations. This third condition is therefore about having the right object of intention instead of being sidetracked by thinking, "This system is true and that system is false."

Proximate Condition

The proximate condition for making success on the path of the preliminary practices is about overcoming hope and fear. You are not to entertain thoughts of meditation and a meditator when you engage in mahamudra. You should not regard meditation as something you have to do and think, "I've just had a pleasant meditation session," or "I've just had an unpleasant session." Do not desire a quiet and peaceful meditation or fear your meditation might be agitated. Do not entertain any such thoughts. You should only be concerned about learning how to rest the mind in its natural condition without contrivances. This condition relates to being free from hope or fear: hope for meditative equipoise or fear of mental agitation.

These four conditions are necessary for the mahamudra experience to occur. The same is true of our sensory experiences. When you perceive an object, there first has to be the causal condition of the visual sense consciousness. The subjective condition is the eye organ, the objective condition is the sensory object, and the instantaneous condition is the coming together of these factors. When these four conditions are present, you perceive an object. In a similar way, the four conditions just elaborated upon must be present if you are to have the meditative experience of mahamudra. Briefly speaking, the mind that is inclined towards the Dharma by being free of temporal and immediate worldly concerns is the causal condition, being in contact with a qualified teacher is the subjective condition, the meditative practices are the objective condition, and trying to free yourself from thought of hope or fear regarding your meditative experiences is the instantaneous condition. A meditator should ensure these four conditions are all present when following mahamudra instructions.

The Actual Practice of Mahamudra

Shamatha

We now come to mahamudra practice proper, which consists of shamatha and vipashyana meditation. *Shamatha* or "tranquility meditation" will be explained in two stages—the general characteristics and the specific characteristics.

General Characteristics

The general characteristics of shamatha consist in learning how to establish the right physical and mental posture so that we can stabilize our meditation.

Physical Posture

You must ensure your body is correctly aligned so that you are meditating with the proper posture. Sit in a cross-legged position with your hands resting upon each other on your lap or resting on their respective knees. Your shoulders should be slightly stretched and your head inclined slightly forwards. Your spine should be absolutely straight, like an arrow. Cast your glance downward so that you are concentrating on the tip of your nose and keep your mouth slightly open with the tip of your tongue touching the roof of your mouth. Your breathing should be even and relaxed. This posture is very important to maintain. While holding this posture, remember these three things: the body should not feel any tension, the body should not feel any heaviness, and the body should not feel any pain. The *Hevajra tantra* says:

> It is important to maintain the proper posture
> Because that will control your level of mental agitation.

The first Karmapa, Dusum Khyenpa says:

> The body and mind are intrdependent, so when the proper physical posture is maintained, it will automatically have an effect on your mind.

The ability to maintain a proper posture makes it easier to maintain a nonagitated state of mind. In addition to maintaining a proper physical posture, you should learn to rest the mind. The mind becomes stabilized by working with your body, which is why so many kinds of yogic exercise are presented in the tantric tradition. It is said that when you train the body, your bodily energy flow will be enhanced, and an unobstructed energy flow makes sure that the mind is balanced. Make sure your spine is straight while sitting, because a body that is leaning either forward, backward, or sideways makes it difficult to maintain concentration.

According to the tantric teachings, thoughts ride on the energy flow. The energy flow circulates throughout the body, so when perfect posture is maintained, the energy flow becomes stabilized. When your body's energy flow is stabilized, your mind also becomes stable. This is the view of both Saraha and Naropa, two great mahamudra masters.

You can also do certain breathing exercises to calm your mind. For example, you could breathe out through your nostrils and think that all your tensions, worries, and anxieties are leaving your body. When you inhale, you should think of inhaling calmness, peace, and tranquility. If you do these practices when you are learning to meditate, it will help to calm the mind.

According to the tantric teachings, there are other reasons for holding a perfect posture. It is said that if you sit in a cross-legged position, the energy flow or *prana* is unblocked and will enter into the central energy pathway and pacify the conflicting emotion of anger. This particular energy is called the "downward moving energy." Resting your arms in your lap directs what is known as the "water element energy" into the central energy pathway, which pacifies the conflicting emotion of jealousy. Having a straight spine ensures the "earth element energy" enters the central energy pathway, which pacifies the conflicting emotion of ignorance. Having the head tilted slightly forwards ensures the "fire element energy" will enter into the central energy pathway, which pacifies the conflicting emotion of grasping and clinging. Casting your glance downward without closing your eyes while having the tip of your tongue touching the roof of your mouth directs the "wind element energy" into the central energy pathway, which pacifies the conflicting emotion of pride.

The tantric teachings also say the five elements and the way energy circulates in the body correspond to the five conflicting emotions, each emotion having the quality of one of the five elements. When the energy circulation occurs properly, the mind also becomes more balanced. Furthermore, the energy travels through the energy pathways and all of the energy pathways are rooted in the eye organ, so having a proper gaze is extremely important for inducing a proper meditative state.

The importance of a proper physical posture cannot be underestimated. You will detect a marked improvement in meditation if you maintain a good posture. You will also notice if your posture is held incorrectly as you will experience an increase in mental agitation. If the body inclines to the right, there may be an experience of mental clarity at the beginning, but you will gradually experience extreme mental agitation. If your body inclines to the left, there may be a certain experience of well-being and relaxation at the beginning, but after a while you could experience intense sexual desire. If your body is leaning forwards, your mind may be relatively calm and free of agitation at the beginning, but this will soon turn into drowsiness and stupor. Furthermore, it is said that this leads to paranoid reactions. For example, if two people are talking, you will start to think, "They are talking about me." The habitual practice of leaning forward while meditating could also produce extreme anxiety reactions of tightness in the chest, difficulty breathing and so on. If you are leaning backwards, your may be initially quite spacious, but this would soon turn into the emotional conflict of pride. If you maintain this sort of posture, it could lead to a loss of weight and nocturnal emissions. In brief, you should try to maintain a proper posture while meditating and make sure every aspect of the posture is correct.

Mental Posture

You should also learn to stabilize your meditation. The perfect posture of shamatha has to be supported by a stable mind, which is cultivated by resting in the present moment without anticipating the future or dwelling in the past. Nothing is gained by dwelling in the past, because what has happened has happened, and one cannot undo or relive it. As for the future, there is no way of knowing what will happen. There is no certainty whatsoever so there is no point worrying about it. You should focus your mind solely on the present experience, without entertaining any thoughts about whether it is good or bad or making any other kind of evaluative judgments. Just allow the experience, whatever is, to be left alone.

This is not, strictly speaking, a mahamudra type of meditation. When you engage in the proper practice of mahamudra meditation, you do not think about time in terms of past, present, and future. However, when you are learning to cultivate concentration, it is helpful to think in terms of focusing your mind on the present, rather than anticipating the future or dwelling in the past. In mahamudra meditation, you do not think in terms of time at all. This is the way you should gradually learn to concentrate.

While cultivating concentration in this way, you should be aware of two things. The first is not to try too hard to concentrate, because that will increase the tension in your mind. You should not think, "I have to concentrate; I have to do this." If you try too hard, your mind will just become tenser. It is important to concentrate, but your mind should also be relaxed. The second is to maintain a sense of mindfulness, even in postmeditation when you are not formally meditating. While eating, try to be mindful of each spoonful of food you place in your mouth. When walking, try to be aware of each step you take. You should gradually try to maintain this mindfulness, even in extreme situations and circumstances that may elicit violent reactions from you. Gampopa says:

> When learning to meditate, you should not dwell in the past or anticipate the future, just focus your mind on its present mental state. "Not dwelling in the past," means not following your thoughts. If you follow your thoughts, you will find that one thought just leads to another and you try to recapture each thought as it passes. "Not anticipating the future," means not

thinking about things that have not yet happened and giving rise to a proliferation of thoughts about future possibilities. "Focusing on the present state of the mind" means being aware of whatever arises in the mind at any given moment. It is said:

> When present experiences are not
> interfered with,
> They automatically become lucid and free
> from agitation,
> Just as a pond is clear if it is left alone
> And becomes muddied by sentiment if it is
> stirred.

For this reason, allow present experience to be there without interference and without imposing any evaluative judgments on them. Furthermore, if you can maintain this concentration for a long time, do not think, "Well done, I've been able to meditate properly this time." If you fail to maintain your concentration, do not become anxious and think, "The meditation has not worked," or "I am unable to meditate." Just relax with whatever thought arises. As it is said:

> If the mind that is twisted into knots is
> loosened
> It will become liberated.

When a thought arises in the mind, simply let that thought go, because when a thought is let go, the mind remains in a state of meditation without trying. If you can learn to let go of thoughts, you will automatically be in a meditative state.

Dombey Heruka's instructions to Gampopa say:

> Do not disturb the mind with judgments of good or bad, just rest the mind like a still pond. Meditate without blocking your sensory impressions, like the sun unobstructed by clouds.

Maintain your mindfulness even in postmeditation—when eating, walking, sitting, lying down, and sleeping. Do not engage in any kind of analysis to try to find out what mind is, what thoughts are, what concepts are. You should try to have direct, unmediated experience. Without trying to grasp or cling to a meditative state and without trying to concentrate too hard, simply allow your mind to rest in the meditative state rather than trying to create it. Furthermore, if mental agitation does arise in the mind, let it go instead of judging it to be disturbing or seeing it as an obstacle to meditation. Saraha says:

> The agitated mind, if left alone, becomes peaceful.

He also says:

> When mind is left alone, insight will occur spontaneously. When mind is conditioned into in a meditative state, it is impossible to attain enlightenment.

If you can gradually learn to let the mind rest without interference, your gross level of thoughts will start to subside and your mind will become more lucid and clear. Achieving this state is called the "meditation of tranquility." It is called tranquility or shamatha, because the gross levels of emotional conflicts have subsided. In Tibetan, tranquility meditation is called *zhi gnas*. *Zhi* means "pacification of emotional conflicts" and *gnas* means "dwelling in that state." It is the same thing as *samadhi*, which is *ting nge 'dzin* in Tibetan. *Ting nge* means "nonwavering" and *'dzin* means "not letting go," so *ting nge 'dzin* means "being in a state of nonagitation or nonwaveringness."

It is a mistake to think the mind should be controlled when meditating and that if the mind is not controlled, it will wander all over the place. From the mahamudra point of view, you should not think that way. A person who has been put behind bars will always think about how to escape, while a person who has the freedom to wander around has no such desire. In the same way, if you try to control your mind, it will react and become even more agitated. The technique is not to control the mind, but to learn to focus it on present experience.

This can be done by simply focusing on a thought as it arises in the mind. Instead of suppressing thoughts or thinking they should not arise, focus your mind on the thought. If you can do this, your thoughts will automatically disperse as they arise instead of becoming agitated. When you are learning to meditate and training in the practice of tranquility, just try to sit for short periods, by doing more sessions but of less duration. The benefit of focusing the mind on your present thoughts is that to realize the nature of thought is to realize the nature of mind, and to realize the nature of mind is the same as to attain mahamudra. In addition, to realize the nature of thoughts makes it possible to eradicate karmic traces and dispositions or habit-forming thoughts. Saraha says:

> Just like a cattle herder lets his cows wander,
> Let the mind roam about freely.

You may come to a point where you have a simple experience of awareness without thinking of this or that. That experience of naked awareness is the same as realizing the nature of mind. As you become more proficient at it, you should lengthen the duration of your meditation sessions.

This is something you should gradually become accustomed to rather than forcing yourself to meditate for long periods. Also, it is important to maintain mindfulness in daily life. As you become more proficient at meditation, it will become easier to maintain mindfulness in your daily activities.

The result of this practice is a feeling of satisfaction, an experience of well-being, an increased mental clarity and awareness, more enthusiasm for various activities, joy in whatever you experience and delight in meditation. In brief, many kinds of meditative experiences can arise from the practice of tranquility and to have those experiences is a sign that you have established yourself in shamatha. We learn to pacify emotional conflicts through tranquility meditation in this way and this pacification is necessary for the realization of mahamudra.

Specific Characteristics

The general methods of shamatha are about learning to stabilize your meditation. However, once your mind has become stabilized, you must learn to maintain that stability. The stabilization of shamatha is cultivated through three techniques: stabilizing the agitated mind, strengthening that stabilization by dealing with the obscurations of stupor and mental agitation, and actualizing that mental stability.

Stabilizing the Agitated Mind

There are three main techniques for stabilizing the agitated mind: using an external object, not using any specific object, and using the breath.

Using an External Object

You can use gross physical objects, such as scenery or a road, or anything else present in your visual field to stabilize the mind. The important thing is to maintain a connection between your visual experience and consciousness so that they do not become disengaged. You can also use smaller objects such as a piece of wood or a pebble, to develop concentration and stabilize the mind by simply focusing your mind on that object.

The importance of not focusing on the meditative object too intently should be emphasized here. You need to restrain your mind from wandering away from the meditation object, but you should also maintain a sense of relaxation. Do not analyze the object by thinking, "This is a short piece of wood" or "this is a thick piece of wood," and so on. Simply make a phenomenological observation of the visual object. The function of the meditative object is to enhance your concentration. Simply be aware of the object, rather than grasping onto it or trying to focus on it too intently. An element of relaxation is extremely important here. You should not mistake the object of meditation for the function of meditation. The function of meditation is not to concentrate on a piece of wood or any other object.

While focusing on such an object, your vision may sometimes blur or you may have the feeling the object has moved and so on. You should then stop focusing on that object and gaze straight ahead into space and then relax in that state. Do not direct your mind to any particular object, but maintain a simple awareness, so that your mind does not fall under the influences of stupor and drowsiness. If you are able to maintain this awareness, the mind will become lucid and you will experience mental ease. However, if you become too concerned with maintaining your meditative equipoise and eliminating disturbing thoughts, you will not be able to maintain a proper meditative state. Therefore, try not to concern yourself with either hope or fear. Lama Shang says:

When you meditate according to the mahamudra instructions, do not strive to attain a meditative state and do not direct your mind to any particular object. A meditative state is not attained by hankering after it. It is not produced by excessive effort. You will not attain mahamudra from either hankering or making too much effort to realize this state.

When meditating, do not make any physical or mental effort or exertion. Instead, let the mind rest without contrivances. Let the mind rest without causing any internal conflict. Let the mind rest in a relaxed manner. Mahamudra experience is not created; it arises spontaneously through being in the right frame of mind. If you know how to let your mind rest in this way, you will no longer be unsettled by disturbing thoughts but will have a sense of spaciousness. When such meditative experiences arise, do not judge them to be indications of progress. If you are unable to maintain this approach for very long, do not judge that as a sign of failure. If you can develop this attitude, disturbing thoughts will reveal the innate nature of mind, which is luminosity. In this way, the mahamudra view is not to desire meditative equipoise or have aversion to emotional conflicts and disturbing thoughts. You should view them both with equanimity.

Gampopa says:

When meditators are learning to stabilize the mind, they should not regard meditative equipoise as something good. If they fail to have an experience of meditative equipoise, they should not regard that is a failure. The important point is not whether meditative equipoise is present, but whether you can maintain awareness in both a settled and a disturbed state of mind. If disturbing thoughts arise, you should use them with awareness to recognize that thoughts are transient—they arise, persist for a while, and then disperse. The transience of a thought is revealed by its elusiveness. Before you can get hold of a thought, it is already gone, and another one has appeared in its place.

Tilopa says:

> Allow the mind to relax in an unconditional state,
> Because when the mind is relaxed, you will achieve liberation.

He also says:

> If you can maintain awareness
> In the states of agitation and meditative equipoise,
> The pollution of disturbing thoughts will clear automatically,
> Just like a pond that is left undisturbed.
>
> Do not consider certain mental experiences
> As good and worth cultivating and other experiences
> As hindrances that need to be abandoned.
> If you can develop this attitude,
> Your mind will gradually be emptied of its unconscious contents:
> The karmic traces and dispositions and all the obscurations.

Gyalwa Gotsangpa says:

> When a disturbing thought arises in the mind,
> Focus your mind on that thought and rest in that state,

> Instead of reacting to it.
> If you can rest on a thought it will be self-liberated.

This is extremely important. Many people think meditation is about learning to control the mind instead of relaxing it. Urgyenpa says:

> If you try to control the mind, it will only get claustrophobic and your agitation will increase, just as silkworms produce the very fibers they become entangled in. The mind should be relaxed but not distracted; there has to be that balance. When you are spinning thread, you should not spin it too taut or it will break and you should not spin it too lose or it will unravel. There should be that same kind of balance in the mind.

In mahamudra, the criterion by which we judge whether we are meditating, is not whether we are exercising control over the mind but whether awareness is present or not. Awareness is more important than controlling the mind. You actually have to learn to relax the mind.

This criterion should to be applied every time you meditate or use any kind of meditation object. Do not regard disturbing thoughts and emotions as something that upsets meditation. Allow them to arise, be aware of them, and let them go. It is possible to meditate on disturbing thoughts themselves with this approach.

There are other methods or ways to cultivate concentration. Gampopa says:

> You can use a lamp that is reflected in a mirror. Instead of concentrating on the lamp, concentrate on its reflection and remain with that meditation object.

You can also use space as an object of meditation. You can

also concentrate on the point between your eyebrows by imagining a white dot the size of a pea. Regardless of the technique you are using, the most important thing is not to analyze the object of meditation, but simply to use it to anchor the mind. If you prefer, you can visualize the Buddha sitting on a throne flanked by lions. Visualize him as golden in color, with one face and two hands, and sitting on a sun-and-moon disk. Visualize the Buddha as exceptionally beautiful and with light radiating from his body. Imagine he is very pleased with you and then concentrate on his image. If drowsiness or stupor arises, try to concentrate more on the upper portion of his body. If agitation arises, concentrate more on the feet and navel areas.

The second technique for cultivating concentration with a meditation object is to use visualization as the object of meditation. In this context, you can visualize a deity or a guru and so on. There are many different methods for this, but they are tantric methods, so they are oriented toward the realization of the nature of mind that is free from all empirical determinations. By relying on mental images, you come to realize that which is devoid of any form. The *Mahayanasutralamkara* says:

> By relying on images,
> We realize that which is formless.

Not Using any Specific Object

We can also use the method of dissolving the physical world through the technique of visualization. Dissolve one element into another, imagining that the physical world is gradually disappearing altogether, and then concentrate on that nothingness.

Using the Breath

This method involves watching the breath by being mindful

of your inhalations and exhalations. You can also count your breath by taking each exhalation, inhalation, and middle period as one breath. You can count a cycle of breaths twenty-one times, eighty times, a hundred times, and so on. When concentrating on the breath, you should focus on the breath coming in and going out on the inside of your nostrils.

We learn to stabilize the mind through using these various techniques and objects of meditation. You will first develop a rudimentary ability to stabilize the mind, which may be followed by awareness of how agitated the mind is and you might feel the proliferation of thoughts has increased since you started to meditate. However, this is not true, this is only a sign you are becoming more aware of what is going on in your mind. Instead of feeling your meditation has been destabilized by this invasion of unceasing thoughts, simply notice them and maintain an awareness of them.

If you can maintain awareness, even while your mind is agitated, those disturbing thoughts will disperse spontaneously, just like snow falling on a warm boulder. If you persist with this practice, you will gradually maintain a meditative state, even when disturbing thoughts arise in the mind and your thoughts become more stabilized, like the gentle flow of a river. When you have a distinct feeling of physical and mental well-being and can maintain a sense of awareness in everyday life, this is the result of being able to maintain mental stability with lucidity, like the stillness of the ocean. This final stability is the attainment of *samadhi* or meditative equipoise. You should learn the nine methods of resting the mind:

1) Resting the mind on a meditative object,
2) Resting the mind by prolonging your attention on that object,

3) Resting the mind on disturbing thoughts without losing awareness,
4) Resting the mind by ensuring awareness is not disrupted,
5) Resting the mind with a sense of delight and joy in that awareness,
6) Applying awareness to detect distractions and the nature of distractions,
7) Applying awareness to detect the causes of distraction and extreme emotion,
8) Resting the mind without needing to make any effort, and
9) Maintaining awareness and preventing distraction without meditating.

Strengthening Stabilization by Overcoming Drowsiness and Mental Agitation

You can strengthen your meditative stabilization with the following visualizations to settle the mind. You should practice these techniques separately and then practice them both in quick succession. Their function is to deal with the obstacle of mental agitation and the obstacle of drowsiness and stupor. You will encounter many obstacles to meditation, but all of them can be subsumed under two categories: drowsiness or stupor, and mental agitation. Other obstacles, such as laziness and so on, must be dealt with by contemplating mortality, the inevitability of death, the dissatisfactory nature of samsara, and the urgency that arises from uncertainty about the time of death, but the two real obstacles to meditation are stupor and mental agitation.

Visualization one: In your heart center, visualize a white four-petaled lotus in the center of which rests a luminous object the size of a pea. Inhale and then eject the luminous object through the crown of you head as you exhale. As it bursts through your crown, it shoots into space, and then rests there above your head, at which point one should expand your chest, gaze upwards, and focus on that luminous object.

Visualization two: In your heart center, visualize a black four-petaled lotus in the center of which rests a black object the size of a pea. This time the lotus is visualized facing downwards. Inhale and then push the black object down and force it into the ground and then rest it there, at which point you should pull your chest inwards, gaze downwards and focus on that black object with a slight sense of heaviness in your body.

If drowsiness or stupor arises, expand your chest, straighten your spine, widen your eyes, and gaze into the distance. It is also helpful to have some water in a container to splash on your face and refresh yourself. Try not to overheat the room or remove some layers of clothing to freshen yourself up. It also helps to shorten your meditation sessions, so instead of sitting for one long session, take a few breaks and divide your time into shorter sessions. If drowsiness and stupor become a recurring problem, cut down on how much you eat and drink and do not sit in the sun or by a fire for too long. You could also engage in physical exercises and breathing exercises or occasionally go for walks while trying to cultivate mindfulness and awareness. If drowsiness and stupor take over, you will not be able to meditate, so applying these methods should help you to gradually overcome them.

If your mind is agitated, try to relax both mind and body. Eat nutritional food, get massages and physical manipulations, and put on a few more layers of clothing. Try to focus your mind on objects that are convenient to use. If your mind becomes too agitated, take a break instead of persisting with the practice and then go back to it. If agitation becomes too intense and difficult to overcome, engage in analysis to see where the disturbing thoughts are coming from and examine their contents. Are the thoughts about trivial daily experiences or are they about your practice or other spiritual concerns?

If your thoughts are about everyday life, think about impermanence and the transient nature of everything, because nothing is certain. For example, if you are feeling anger toward someone or have love for someone, contemplate the nature of impermanence and try to see these feelings as mere judgments of the mind. You can also use the meditation on impermanence for other kinds of worries and concerns. Try to reawaken your commitment by thinking, "Following the spiritual path is not about changing my dress or external appearance, it is about changing my attitudes and transforming my inner being." Ruminate on these thoughts and you will be able to use thoughts to overcome mental agitation.

If disturbing thoughts originate from spiritual concerns, such as agitation over attaining buddhahood or concern over philosophical points, remind yourself that this will not lead to a direct realization of buddhahood. Buddhahood is not attained by thinking about emptiness, the real nature of things and so on; it comes from engaging in proper practice. Meditation is the only way delusions can be overcome. They are not overcome by intellectualizing about reality or the nature of things. Think about the importance of practicing meditation and the limitations of intellectual understanding.

There is a slight difference between stupor and drowsiness. Stupor is a lack of mental clarity where the mind is robbed of lucidity, and drowsiness means you are actually falling asleep, so that even when disturbing thoughts arise, you are not aware of them. You also fail to discriminate between positive and negative meditative experiences.

Vajrasattva practice is useful for combating drowsiness and stupor, because its real source lies in your defilements and any form of purification practice is therefore extremely helpful.

Another helpful method for overcoming both these obstacles is to refrain from using any of the antidotes that were mentioned in previous exercises. Simply use agitation, drowsiness, or stupor themselves as the objects of meditation. Realize that agitation, drowsiness, and stupor are states of mind, and that whatever your mental state, it is inseparable from the nature of mind itself. In this way, without having to abandon either of these mental states, you will realize innate wisdom and gradually overcome these two obstacles to meditation. When you have developed this ability, you might think, "Now I have achieved real meditation" and feel proud. You need to be aware of that danger as well.

Actualizing Mental Stability

Focus your mind on a visual object if you are able and then include all objects in the immediate surrounding area within your awareness. Then focus your mind on a sound, a smell, a physical sensation, or a mental image. Try to focus on each of these sensory impressions one at a time. You can also focus your mind on the emotional conflicts that are generally considered something to be abandoned. You should focus your mind on virtuous thoughts, such as generosity, patience, morality, and so on, and then focus on neutral and trivial thoughts. Try to focus in this way on negative emotions, positive emotions, negative thoughts, positive thoughts, and neutral thoughts. Some people say negative thoughts and emotions cannot be used as objects of meditation because they need to be abandoned. However, from this perspective, trying to abandon negative thoughts and emotions only causes more disturbing thoughts and destabilizes your meditative equipoise.

For this reason, even when a disturbing thought arises, do not view it as harmful. Learn to relax by focusing on that thought without reaction. Instead of trying to stabilize the mind by hanging onto a particular thought, just let your thoughts go and another fresh thought will arise in its place. The functional point of the practice is to maintain mindfulness and awareness. It has nothing to do with blocking thoughts and so on. This is the way to gradually stabilize your mental experiences. Even if you do not experience a stabilization of your thoughts and instead find them becoming even more disturbed, do not feel discouraged and view that as harmful to your meditation. Simply be aware of them, because if you can learn to focus your mind on thoughts properly, they can themselves become meditation. The *Mahayanasutralamkara* says:

> If a skilled practitioner
> Can meditate on negative emotions,
> Such as grasping and anger,
> He or she will achieve liberation;
> There is no uncertainty about that.

The *Hevajra tantra* says:

> Human beings are bound by lust,
> Yet it is possible to achieve enlightenment through that very lust.

Gyalwa Yanggonpa says:

> Do not abandon disturbing thoughts
> Or try to cultivate a state of nonthough,
> Just learn to establish yourself in shamatha through mindfulness.

This quotation also means that negative thoughts and emotions can be used to develop concentration and meditative equipoise. As you continue with shamatha practice, you should practice mindfulness and awareness with intensity for a short time, relax your intensity for a while, and then practice with intensity once again. To practicing mindfulness and awareness more intensely means to focus your awareness on what is going on in the mind, just as you would try to spot an escaped prisoner in a crowd or to walk extra carefully when carrying a pot full of boiling oil. Relaxing your intensity for a while means to cease your vigilance and relax your mind while trying to maintain a general sense of mindfulness and awareness. Try to relax your mind and to feel your body is completely relaxed, and then generate a sense of physical and mental well-being. You should relax the way a pile of straw falls to the ground when its bindings have been cut.

You will gradually learn to deal with the obstacles of stupor and mental agitation in the context of these two practices of intensity and relaxation. However, it is important to keep in mind that you should not get too fixated on these techniques or the order in which you are practicing them. Experiment with your own needs and find out what works best for you.

Many kinds of misunderstandings can arise about meditation practice. For example, when you are told to meditate without trying to create a state of meditative equipoise so that the unconditioned mind arises, or that you should leave your mind alone without trying to abandon disturbing thoughts, you might conclude there is actually no difference between the mind of enlightenment and the ordinary mind of delusion. If you are making this mistake, you should try to improve your understanding of these instructions and attempt to have direct experience of them instead of only a conceptual understanding.

As you continue with the practice, it is important to be aware of the different meditative experiences that will arise in due course, so that they do not reinforce your misconceptions about the nature of actual realization. You might mistakenly think meditative experiences are the same as realizations and become deluded about your own attainments. You can also have various delusions about the meditative experiences themselves and must deal with them with the repeated use of mindfulness and awareness so that you can gain insight into the nature of these experiences.

Vipashyana

The section on *vipashyana* or "insight meditation" will be dealt with in three stages: 1) an explanation of the nature of mind, 2) an analysis of the nature of mind, and 3) introducing the nature of mind to the meditator.

An Explanation of the Nature of Mind

The practice of vipashyana should be preceded by brief periods of contemplation on the ordinary preliminary practices. You should also stabilize the mind in the manner explained in the previous chapter. Rest the mind like the cloudless sun. Rest the mind like waves on the ocean and realize all disturbing thoughts and mental processes are inseparable from the nature of mind itself. Rest the mind with a sense of mental clarity, with no fixation or grasping, like a child admiring a mural.

Once you have rested the mind in this manner, engage in the following meditative thinking, "In what manner does the mind rest? Does mind have color or shape? Is it a material entity or an immaterial one? How does mind come into being? Where does it dwell? Where is it located? How does it cease or does it cease at all?"

Investigate the mind in relation to your body and the external world in this way. Engage in this form of meditative thinking repeatedly. You might occasionally think,

"This is a pointless exercise," but do not be discouraged by these thoughts; just continue with the analysis. If you engage in this kind of meditative thinking, you will gradually come to experience the mind as luminous, yet without any determinable characteristics. To recognize that mind has no inherent existence and yet fully manifest is considered the right view.

Once you have developed sufficient ability to rest the mind, deliberately create thoughts. Try to think of as many things as possible, and then contemplate the way these thoughts come into being and what they are concerned about. Try to determine where these thought are located, by examining your body from top to toe. Look into the relationship between your thoughts and sensory impressions and contemplate on how thoughts came into being.

An Analysis of the Nature of Mind

You analyze the nature of mind by following a series of exercises designed to demonstrate that it is empty yet luminous. Begin by analyzing that which is doing the analysis. Who is engaged in this type of meditative thinking? Who is trying to determine the origin of thoughts? Who is trying to determine the nature of thoughts? Try to determine the differences and similarities between a tranquil state of mind and an agitated state of mind. Contemplate whatever arises in the mind in relation to the three stages of thought: the onset of a thought, the duration of a thought, and the dispersal of a thought. If your mind is in a tranquil state, give rise to one thought, two thoughts, three thoughts, and so on, and try to see the relationship between the bearer of these thoughts and the thoughts themselves. Are they the same? Engage in this meditative thinking in relation to a tranquil state and an agitated state to determine the nature of both.

These analyses can be accomplished by using eleven different methods:

1) Analyzing the mind to determine its nature,
2) Analyzing the specific characteristics of thoughts in terms of their onset, duration and dispersal,
3) Analyzing the relationship between the thought that is being analyzed and the analyzer of that thought,
4) Determining the nature of mind to be empty of substance and thereby understanding that non-mental phenomena are also devoid of substance,
5) Analyzing the relationship between meditative equipoise and the thoughts you have given rise to from within that state,
6) Determining that the state of meditative equipoise and various thought forms have the same nature,
7) Dealing with stupor by contemplating things that activate the mind,
8) Calming the mind through various methods when it is in an agitated state,
9) Determining the nature of mind to be free from mental stupor and agitation,
10) Applying these different methods of analysis in an appropriate manner, and
11) Achieving a meditative state where the mind is no longer disturbed.

We use these different analyses to ensure our vipashyana does not remain a conceptual exercise, but becomes an experiential thing. If you can carry out this analysis in the proper manner, you will realize the nature of mind as empty yet luminous. How that is realized will depend on the personality, predilections, and inclinations of the individual. For some people, this realization will occur instantaneously, while for others it may be a gradual realization, first as glimpses of the nature of mind during shamatha and then as deeper realization at the level of vipashyana and so on.

Furthermore, do not regard the thoughts that arise in the mind as something to be discarded during this analysis. You should use them as part of meditation, because from the mahamudra point of view, the nature of mind is not sought after as something hidden and obscured by thoughts and concepts. To realize the nature of thoughts is the same as to realize the nature of mind. This is why the nature of mind is sometimes called "ordinary mind" or *tha mal gyi shes pa*. If you can recognize the nature of your present state of mind as empty yet luminous, it is the same as realizing the nature of mind. The nature of mind is not realized by abandoning thoughts, nor is it realized by seeking some occult entity you have never experienced; it is this same mind that you immediately experience during insight. When the nature of this same mind is realized, you have realized the nature of mind itself. This is how the insight of vipashyana arises. The nature of mind is perceived as empty yet luminous, because the mind has no abiding substance or essence. It has never been polluted by ignorance and defilement, so it is intrinsically luminous.

You must combine shamatha and vipashyana and examine the nature of mind. If you can examine the nature of mind properly, you will attain self-knowledge. To attain self-knowledge is the same as to realize the wisdom of mahamudrahood. Unless you engage in meditation, you will not gain insight into the nature of mind. If you do not gain insight into the nature of mind, you will not recognize innate wisdom. If you do not recognize innate wisdom, you will not be able to realize the innate wisdom that is supreme bliss itself. You should think about this and continue with your meditation.

Introducing the Nature of Mind to the Meditator

It is not sufficient to have a certain feeling toward meditation or to have a rudimentary sense of being in a meditative state; you must try to deepen that experience and develop certainty in your meditative experience. If you continue with vipashyana, the nature of mind will be revealed as blissful, luminous, unobstructed, expansive, and spacious. Direct realization of this is hard to put into words because the full meaning of it cannot be conveyed through language or concepts. You can nonetheless have this experience by engaging in the following exercises, which are called "introducing the nature of mind to the meditator." This has two stages: introducing the nature of mind while mind is in a state of movement and introducing the nature of mind in relation to the sensory impressions.

Introducing the Nature of Mind while the Mind is in a State of Movement

Exercise One

Begin by contemplating the ordinary preliminaries and then try to relax and develop concentration as described in the shamatha section. While in a state of awareness, focus your mind on your state of relaxation, then give rise to a certain mental image, such as a building, and focus your mind on that. Examine the difference between this and the previous state of meditative relaxation. Examine the difference between the mental image and the aspect of mind that is focusing on that image. If you continue with this practice, you will gradually recognize that everything is conditioned by mind. Any separation you might see is only a projection of the mind itself.

Exercise Two

The next exercise involves thinking of something that you love or that gives you enormous joy, and then increasing this love or joy to the greatest possible degree. Follow this by thinking of something you despise intensely and then develop that dislike to the greatest possible level of intensity. Look into the nature of each of these responses and try to determine whether there is any difference between them. What is the difference between the mind that loves and the mind that despises?

Exercise Three

Look into the similarities or differences between the mind that experiences these intense emotions and the mind of the first exercise that was relatively stable.

Exercise Four

Give rise to as many thoughts as possible and then try to scatter the mind in all directions. What is the difference between the meditative state, the stable mind, and the mind that is scattered?

The upshot of all these exercises is that you realize unity in multiplicity. Even though the mind generates multiplicities of thoughts and images, they all have the same nature, for the simple reason they arise from the same nature of mind.

Exercise Five

Focus the mind on a particular thought, and you will see that simply by focusing on a thought in this way makes it become elusive. You will see that thoughts are not something you can pin down and grasp, and as a result, they will dissipate by themselves. You will realize that disturbing thoughts are not something you have to deliberately abandon, eradicate, or use positive thoughts to counteract.

If you use the right method, whatever binds you can become the thing that frees you. If you develop this skill and use this method, you will become enlightened in this very life. You will be able to use your various negative emotions to reveal the nature of mind. It is not essential to always focus on positive thoughts and emotions.

Exercise Six

Visualize a person that you sexually desire. Increase your lust to the point of almost losing control, and then look into that lust. Think of a person you intensely dislike. Increase your aversion to the point of being unbearable and then look into that hatred. When you feel drowsy or sleepy before going to bed, look into that mind. Look into your pride, jealousy, covetousness, and so on in the same way.

You can practice awareness in relation to all types of experiences and meditative states, without imposing any judgments on them. If you cultivate this awareness without bias, insight will arise and the five poisons will be purified automatically, without your having to abandon them. This is what is meant by the term "self-liberation." When the five poisons are not abandoned but self-liberated, they manifest as the five wisdoms. These five wisdoms are symbolically represented by the tantric iconography of different deities, who all belong to the five Buddha-families, each one of which signifies one of the five wisdoms. This is also called "using the five poisons to further advance on the spiritual path." As a previous mahamudra master says:

> The tantric path possesses the method
> For using the five poisons on the path
> Without having to abandon them.

In brief, in terms of your good, bad, and neutral karma, if you realize there is nothing to abandon and nothing that requires an antidote because it is all devoid of enduring essence; that is the attainment of self-knowledge. This is the same as actualizing the innate wisdom of nonduality. All the delusions that have obscured the innate wisdom up to this point become self-liberated. Gampopa says:

> The nature of thoughts is dharmakaya.
> The only antidote you need in meditation is non-interference.
> Awareness is attained from the lucidity of mind.

Maitreyanatha says:

> The mind does not need to be made more lucid
> Or deliberately put to rest.
> Simply focus on the innate nature of mind
> And you will become liberated through this recognition.

Gyalwa Gotsangpa says:

> When a thought arises in the mind,
> Do not view it as bad.
> If you recognize the nature of thoughts to be emptiness,
> Thoughts are realized as dharmakaya.

Many more quotations of this nature could be used to support the view that disturbing thoughts and negative emotions are not something we deliberately need to abandon; we simply need to understand their nature. It is only that you have not been able to use thoughts as part of your meditation in the past. We learn to use thoughts to attain a meditative state in the methods of the mahamudra teachings. Eyes never look at themselves; they always look outward. In a similar way, our disturbing thoughts have been opaque up to this point. Through the mahamudra method, thoughts become translucent, and when we realize their nature, we will no longer be disturbed by anything that happens in the mind. Whatever arises in the mind, regardless of its content, we will recognize its nature and no longer react to it from either fear or hope. We will simply be able to allow those mental processes to occur and our thoughts and emotions will become self-liberated. Gampopa says:

> Do not think of suppressing thoughts, but instead think how wonderful, how beneficial, and how indispensable it is to have disturbing thoughts, because without them, how would you recognize the nature of mind?

You should not think you have to abandon your thoughts. It is just that, up this point, you have not understood the nature of your thoughts. That is the cause of your samsaric condition. If you use the right method, thoughts can reveal the nature of mind, which is the dharmakaya. For this reason, you should regard your thoughts as a useful and indispensable means for realizing the dharmakaya and gaining insight into the nature of the mind. Gampopa says:

> All problems in meditation are created by thinking that thoughts are harmful and need to be abandoned. Many meditators have become lost through thinking they have to overcome disturbing thoughts. It is very difficult to overcome thoughts, so this mistaken notion creates enormous hardships for them.

Instead of thinking disturbing thoughts are bad and to be

discarded, you should think the more thoughts you have in your mind, the more ferocious and intense will be the fire of wisdom, just as a forest fire blazes more strongly when it is densely populated by trees. Disturbing thoughts and negative emotions are the fuel for the fire of wisdom. This is what the previous masters meant when they said "ordinary human beings do not recognize they are buddhas." To know this is to realize buddhahood. Phagmo Drugpa says:

> Disturbing thoughts are the cause of awareness, so focus your mind on them with a sense of joy. You thoughts will only become more prolific if you try to eradicate them, but if you realize they have no enduring essence, there will be no need to abandon them.

By realizing that disturbing thoughts and the nature of mind are the same, you realize the absolute guru, which is within yourself. In this way, a mahamudra practitioner does not try to abandon disturbing thoughts or cultivate nonconceptual wisdom, but sees wisdom and thoughts as indivisible, just like the water and the saltiness of the ocean are inseparable. Thoughts are the inner guru, because they guide us to realize the innate nature of mind. Many masters have said:

> Try not to hanker after a peaceful meditative state that is relaxed and spacious, but use whatever arises in the mind as part of meditation.

The key point here is to use awareness, no matter what arises in the mind, without trying to condition the mind. Just as the reflection of the moon in water and the water are not separable, everything that occurs in the mind is not separable from the nature of mind. The nature of mind is not found elsewhere and it is not found by abandoning your mental processes; they are the same. This is how we realize the dharmakaya. Another image for this is the inseparability of the ocean and its waves. The emotions and thoughts that arise in the mind and the nature of mind are equally inseparable. The *Hevajra tantra* says:

> This same condition is sometimes called "samsara" and sometimes called "nirvana" because nirvana is not obtained by abandoning samsara.

In this way, we have to realize that everything is in the mind. You should persist with vipashyana practice and contemplate your various thoughts and emotions; your experiences of pain and pleasure, unhappiness and happiness, friends that give you joy and enemies that cause you distress. Who is the creator of all this? Is there some external creator, like the god Brahma, who is responsible for all these experiences? If there is such a being, where does it dwell? When did it create the experiences of human beings? What is meant by the experiences of human beings being created by some external being? What is the manner of that creation?

If you come to the conclusion there is no such external creator but that your own mind is actually responsible for all your experiences, you should look into whether there is any separation between the activities of the mind and the mind itself. You will gradually realize that your own mind is responsible for all your experiences; it is the creator of both samsara as well as nirvana. You will also see that this deluded mind is transient and nonabiding. Our karmic impressions have made us create the perception of various world forms. We then have a perception of the external world through our sensory impressions. The activities of mind and the mind are therefore the same; they are not different. The various mental acts and the mind itself are one and the same thing. The *Vajrapanjara* says:

> There is no such thing
> As ordinary sentient beings and buddhas outside the mind.
> We can speak of nothing outside our human experience;
> Everything is within the realm of mind.

Saraha says:

> The mind is the sole creator of everything that exists.
> The samsaric and nirvanic conditions
> Are reflected in the mind.

The mind is the source of all our suffering and woe. It is also the treasure from which we will gain all our wealth. When the mind becomes transformed, our perception of the world becomes transformed. We cannot speak of reality as existing independently of mind.

Introducing the Nature of Mind in Relation to the Sensory Impressions

This introduction to the nature of mind will be done in four stages: revealing the sensory impressions to be dependent on mind, revealing the nature of mind to be emptiness, revealing emptiness to be spontaneously arisen, and revealing the spontaneously arisen to be self-liberated.

Revealing the Sensory Impressions to be Dependent on Mind

The meditator is introduced to phenomena by contemplating sensory impressions and determining the phenomenal world to be conditioned by mind. Begin this practice by first contemplating the four preliminaries for a brief period and then practicing shamatha meditation. After some time, you should focus your mind on a visual object. While focusing on the visual object, try to see if there is any gap between the visual object and the mind. Examine the way the visual object is being apprehended. Does the physical object impress itself on the mind or is the mind actively imposing certain categories upon the raw data of the sense impressions? Contemplate on the rest of the sensory impressions in this way as well.

If you persist with this practice of observing the sense objects phenomenologically, you will realize there is no separate and distinct mind apart from the apprehension of the sense objects, and you will come to realize that all sensory impressions are conditioned by the mind. The *Lankavatara sutra* says:

> Our perceptions of the external world are determined by our karmic traces and dispositions. Even though we might mistakenly believe in an external material world that exists independently of mind, in reality, that is not so.

Do the same exercise to establish the relationship between body and mind. Contemplate the relationship between body and mind by asking, "Are body and mind the same?" "Is the body some kind of host for the mind?" "Are the physical sensations experienced by the body or are they experienced by the mind?" If you continue with this practice, you will realize there can be no "body" outside of your mental experience. We cannot conceive of a body dissociated from the mind.

These exercises help us to realize "the inseparability of mind and phenomena." The seemingly external and independent physical world is dependent on the workings of the human mind. It has no independent existence apart from that. We gradually come to realize "unity in diversity." Even though mind seems to experience an external world in its various forms and mind experiences its own variety of mental processes, they are all imbued with the same reality, and that reality is the nature of mind.

This is the view that does not fall into the extremes of eternalism or nihilism. The right view avoids the extreme of seeing things as unity or seeing things as diversity. We instead see that everything is a combination of unity and diversity, just like the reflections of the moon and the stars on water. There may be many different reflections on the water, but they are all reflected on the same water. We cannot separate the water from the diversity of reflections. We can also perceive this unity and diversity in relation to the external world. In mahamudra, this insight is established purely by examining the mind. We do not need to examine external objects, as in the traditional mahayana teachings. Urgyenpa says:

> The mind and the diversity of the external world are
> united,
> Just as fire is united with heat.

Our perception of the phenomenal world is regarded as a reflection of the mind rather than something totally separate from the mind. Gampopa says:

> The perception of the external world is dependent on the mind. We cannot find a material world that exists totally separately from the mind. The material world is a reflection of the mind rather than an independently existing thing. If your understanding of this leads you to realize the nature of mind, you will

automatically realize the nature of the external world. It is not necessary to separately examine the nature of the world. We realize the nature of the external world through realizing the nature of mind because of unity in diversity. This is the same as the realization of non-dual wisdom.

Lama Shang says:

> The nature of mind is dharmakaya and the phenomenal world is a reflection of that dharmakaya. Not only are the modulations in the mind a product of mind, our perception of the external world is also a product of mind. Even our experiences of samsara and nirvana are conditioned by mind.

All the diversities of samsaric and nirvanic phenomena are united in one source: the mind. This is comparable to many small rivers all joining together in the Ganges and then flowing down to the ocean to be imbued with one flavor, the flavor of salt. One-flavoredness signifies that unity is present in diversity; there is the flavor of the unity within the diversity.

For example, we may have all kinds of disturbing thoughts in our minds but none of them has any enduring essence. They all have the nature of emptiness, so there is unity in diversity there as well.

Je Gotsangpa says:

> You must realize the external world is a reflection of the mind itself, just like reflections in a mirror or reflections of the moon and stars in water. We do not have to renounce the external world; we need

to learn not to become fixated on it. If you can relinquish your fixation in this way, you will attain mahamudrahood.

When you gain a proper appreciation of this, you will realize the "inseparability of the phenomenal world and emptiness" and the "inseparability of emptiness and the nature of mind." Once you recognize this, no matter what experiences you have, they will all become self-purifying and self-liberating.

When you focus your mind on either external sensory impressions or on internal mental processes, you do not need to eradicate the multiplicity, you simply need to realize unity in diversity, by understanding all of your experiences are reflections of the nature of mind. You can then use any experience as part of meditation. For example, if you are ill, you can meditate on that. If you are hungry, you can meditate on that. If you are cold, you can meditate on that. If you are in distress, you can meditate on that. If you are happy, you can meditate on that.

In brief, nothing is anathema to the practice of meditation. Anything and everything can be of use, because all these experiences occasion the opportunity to realize the nature of mind. You cannot find the dharmakaya apart from mind. The dharmakaya is not some transcendental entity; it is the same as the realization of the nature of mind.

Urgyenpa says:

Whatever you perceive through your senses, contemplate on that experience and suspend all your

> judgments. Do not grasp or fixate on these sensory impressions, but observe them in a phenomenological way. This involves focusing your mind on the sensory impressions and perceiving the sensory objects as they are, without any judgments or interpretations. The multiplicity of the phenomenal world does not have to be rejected, and emptiness does not have to be sought after as something separate. We realize unity in diversity, because we realize all multiplicities have the same flavor.

Kyobpa Drikungpa says:

> The multiplicity of experiences in samsara and nirvana is united in the unborn nature of mind itself.

This is how you will realize the indivisibility of emptiness and the phenomenal world as well as the indivisibility of emptiness and the nature of mind. This is the same as the realization of nonduality.

Revealing the Nature of the Mind to be Emptiness

The nature of mind is said to be empty yet luminous, but this should not mislead you into thinking the mind has some color or shape or is an entity of any kind. Mind is not an entity; it is more akin to space than anything else. As mentioned in some of the previous exercises, when you try to discover whether mind has any empirical characteristics, you will fail to find anything there. When mind is not examined in this way, you may mistake it for an entity amongst other entities, but when you try to locate the mind and identify what it is, you will fail to find any such characteristics or any such entity. Mind is elusive, but there is still a mind. We fail to find it because it cannot be found to exist with any determinate characteristics.

To realize that mind is not something that can be found and identified is to gain insight. Insight does not come from finding the mind, but from failing to find anything called "mind" with any definable attributes or characteristics. It is only through a lack of insight into the mind that we have projected a concept of an enduring self. This mistaken notion leads to the emotional conflicts of grasping, clinging, hatred, and resentment; all kinds of confusions arise from this. This is the root cause of the samsaric condition, a condition that is imbued with dissatisfaction and lack of fulfillment. You should think, "What method can I use to reverse this process?" You will see that the only way to bring this process to an end is to cut it at the root of the problem, and that root is in the mind.

It is important to realize that mind and the concept of a self are not enduring entities. To realize that mind is empty of all empirical characteristics and devoid of any enduring essence is to realize the nature of mind. This insight will help you to understand the nature of the self as well. If you can realize this, you will also realize the nature of physical things to be empty of enduring essence. The result of understanding that emptiness is the nature of both the mental and physical realms is that you will no longer generate conflicting emotions in response to situations.

Revealing Emptiness to be Spontaneously Arisen

Even though the nature of mind is empty, mind is still dynamic and creative rather than static and passive, because mind is a process of unceasing mental activities. This conjunction of emptiness and the unceasing flow of mental events is called the "indivisibility of appearance and emptiness" or the "indivisibility of emptiness and awareness." You should realize that even the material world is imbued with emptiness and not think the material world is one thing and emptiness another. Emptiness is the reality of the material world; they are coexistent. Since reality is all-encompassing, how could there be anything outside it? Emptiness pervades both samsara and nirvana.

"Spontaneously arisen" refers to the indivisibility of the material world and emptiness. They are not found separately, so you cannot underestimate the appearance of the material world or exaggerate the reality of emptiness. Everything you perceive in the mental and physical realms arises because of emptiness. It is called "spontaneously arisen" because emptiness is not dependent upon any causes or conditions. Things can only be brought into being due to causes and conditions because they are empty of inherent existence.

Revealing the Spontaneously Arisen to be Self-Liberated

From beginningless time, the material world is the objective side, consciousness is the subjective side, and emptiness is the nature of both. These three have arisen in harmonious coexistence, and this coexistence is a spontaneously established fact. Within that state of harmony, everything exists in a state of equality because everything is imbued with the same reality of emptiness.

On this level, nothing needs to be discarded or abandoned and nothing needs to be cultivated or developed. Everything exists in perfection within the reality that is emptiness. In that state, all negativities are self-liberated, because there is no hope or fear. There is no fear of being corrupted by emotional conflicts and no hope of striving to achieve liberation. Everything is perceived as one-flavored. If you contemplate this, you will understand the primordial purity of all you experience, both mentally and in the phenomenal world. That is called the "insight of vipashyana."

To gain the insight of vipashyana properly, it is not sufficient to have some understanding of the nature of mind, or some understanding of emptiness, or some understanding of the indivisibility of emptiness and awareness or of emptiness and the phenomenal world. You must have proper understanding of the harmonious coexistence of all three. It must become a direct experience. That direct experience would not be the same as this description of it, because direct experience goes beyond words and concepts. The proper insight of vipashyana is only attained by realizing unbiased, discriminating wisdom. You realize that emptiness is like space, which accommodates all and sundry without discrimination. To bring this home to meditators, Tilopa says:

> We cannot identify the nature of space
> As having this or that attribute
> Or as having this or that empirical characteristic.
> It has no color, shape, or form
> And cannot be contaminated by anything that
>   occurs within it.
> In the same way, emptiness—
> Which is inexorably bound with the mind—
> Is free from all empirical characteristics.
> The nature of mind is not contaminated
> By karma of either a positive or negative nature.

He also says:

> People say that space is empty,
> But that is just a designation.
> We cannot identify space as anything
> Since it is devoid of characteristics.
> In the same way,
> The nature of mind is said to be luminous,
> But the nature of mind
> Cannot be attributed any definable characteristics.
>
> The nature of mind is just like space,

And emptiness is all encompassing.
Nothing is left out of it, nothing is extrinsic to it.

Saraha says:

Realize the nature of mind,
Because it is at the root of both samsaric suffering
And nirvanic bliss.
When you realize this,
Rest the mind without meditating,
Because only deluded people seek enlightenment
By abandoning their own minds.

Shantarakshita says:

Within emptiness, everything exists in a harmonious state,
Whether it is good, bad, beautiful, or ugly.
Just as all the oceans have the flavor of salt,
The diversity of things participates in the unity of emptiness.

Nyima Tsal says:

Everything is a creation of the mind,
And mind is something that cannot be identified as this or that.
When you realize this, you cut the root of samsara and nirvana.
That is the realization of dharmakaya.

Dombipa says:

Samsara and nirvana are not mutually exclusive,
So anyone who hankers after one and abandons the other

Is enduring unnecessary labor.
The body and mind are inseparable,
So to see them as separate is the result of delusion.
The nature of mind is the dharmakaya,
So to divide mind into delusions and wisdom is
pitiable.

Strengthening the Practice

After receiving the meditation instructions, you have to practice them, but you may encounter various obstacles to your progress in meditation. You may also develop faults in your practice. It is important to know how to enhance the positive results of your practice and to remove the faults and hindrances to your progress. This chapter will be presented in four sections: 1) abandoning the five wrong views, 2) developing the three skills, 3) avoiding deviations associated with the view of emptiness, 4) removing the obstacles to practice.

Abandoning the Five Wrong Views

Various misconceptions can arise during practice and these instructions on the five wrong views should be used to dispel such confusions.

Wrong View of the Object

It is wrong to view the three poisons as something that needs to be abandoned and the virtuous qualities as something that needs to be cultivated and thereby having aversion towards the so-called "poisons" and becoming attached to and clinging onto the virtues or sublime qualities. In mahamudra, the three poisons must be used on the path. The mahamudra view is that the poisons and the qualities of wisdom ultimately have the same nature, which is emptiness. In the practice of mahamudra, your mind should not be disturbed by thinking about the things you should renounce and the things you should develop and possess, because thinking in this manner is a subtle form of mental agitation. The past masters say:

> You could engage in the practice of worship for thousands of years, but this will not lead to self-realization.

This approach should not lead you to think you should disregard the functions of karma altogether. You must still give serious consideration to karma; however, your behavior should no longer be governed by the extreme conceptual rigidity of viewing certain actions to be intrinsically good and others to be intrinsically harmful.

In brief, on the relative level, you have to realize there is duality. The diversity of things necessitates certain things you must do and certain things you should refrain from doing. However, on the ultimate level, all dualities and diversities are immersed in the same reality and this reality is realized through nondual wisdom. Purify your mind of the wrong view regarding the object in this way.

Wrong View of the Notion of Time

Mahamudra practitioners should not project their spiritual goals into the distant future by thinking, "If I do this or that practice, I may become enlightened at some time in the distant future." The past, present, and future have to be seen as united in the same reality. Meditators in the mahamudra tradition must remain fully in the present, so do not think of time in terms of past, present and future; the three times are united. Instead of seeing past, present, and future as discontinuous, see them as forming a complete whole and think of realizing mahamudrahood right now in the present.

Wrong View of the Concept of Identity

In many religious systems, and Buddhist schools as well, our ordinary consciousness is said to be deluded and therefore incapable of leading us to spiritual realization. They advise us to gradually transcend ordinary consciousness and develop a transcendental state of consciousness to attain our spiritual goal. According to mahamudra, this duality between deluded empirical consciousness and a pure and uncorrupted transcendental consciousness is mistaken. Deluded consciousness and nondeluded consciousness are one and the same mind. We cannot speak of lower and higher forms of consciousness, ordinary and transcendental forms of consciousness, and so on. The same consciousness that is deluded is also capable of being realized. Lama Shang says:

> Fires burn in firewood,
> Lotuses blossom in mud
> And crops grow from manure.
> If you abandon the deluded mind,
> There is no nondeluded mind to be attained
> elsewhere.

All five wisdoms are present within this same deluded mind. Mind by nature is cognizant of things, which is mirrorlike wisdom. Mind is empty of inherent existence, which is the wisdom of equanimity. Mind is an unceasing dynamic process, which is the wisdom of discrimination. Mind encompasses both samsara and nirvana, which is the wisdom of reality. When we realize the nature of this mind, we become completely free and can do things we were previously unable to do, which is the wisdom of accomplishment. The various expressions of nondeluded mind in different forms of wisdoms are inseparable from mind. The empirical deluded consciousness and the transcendental nondeluded consciousness do not have separate identities. It is the same identity.

Wrong View of the Concept of Nature

We should not think the nature of human beings and the nature of enlightened beings is somehow different. As the past masters say, "Without sentient beings there are no buddhas." Sentient beings have the capacity and the potential to become enlightened. The condition of sentient beings is comparable to a poor person in a ramshackle house who does not know there is a lump of gold under the foundations. He seeks his livelihood from an external source without making use of the wealth that is already there. All the qualities of an enlightened being are already there in an ordinary person. These qualities remain as potentials, but to become enlightened simply means to actualize these potentials rather than to become a completely different person. The *Sambhuta tantra* says:

> Buddha resides within your own body;
> You cannot find buddha elsewhere.
> However, deluded ones keep seeking buddha
> Outside themselves.

It also says:

> Ordinary worldlings
> Keep on seeking buddha everywhere except within.
> They don't realize that buddha is the same as their own mind.

The *Atyayajnana sutra* says:

> If you realize the nature of mind, you have already

> become a buddha. There is no need to seek buddha elsewhere.

Many statements of this nature can be cited from the texts by past masters.

Wrong View of Insight

This mistaken notion involves thinking that insight comes purely from learning rather than discovering it from within. For this reason, many people think that the more learned they become and the more they sharpen their intellect, the more they will be able to understand spiritual matters. However, insight is not gained purely from learning. Dongpopo says:

> Buddhahood is not attained
> Through learning and sharpening your intellect.
> That would be comparable to a person
> Being carried along in the strong currents of a river
> And dying from thirst.

A person of great learning who does not meditate is no better than the person in this simile. Lama Shang says:

> Real insight arises spontaneously from within.
> It does not come from skillfulness in examination
> Or from great learning.
> It cannot be attained through the power of reasoning.

He also says:

> Insight has to arise of its own accord.
> For this reason, engage in meditation and let the mind rest.

Do not become too dependent on your skill in reasoning, your level of learning, or whether your intellect is dull or sharp. Do not be held back by your traumatic and upsetting experiences or because you possess great diligence. Insight will not necessarily arise from any of these means. Insight arises from practice, from being in the right frame of mind, and from receiving the proper instructions. Unless the mind has been trained through the practice of meditation and made supple and workable thereby, no amount of activities or means will lead to direct insight. Past masters say:

> Insight arises in someone who has humility and who has practiced training the mind. It arises in the midst of deluded thoughts; it arises from the depths of conflicting emotions. This kind of realization arises from the center of meditative experiences.

Meditate on the five wrong views so that you gain a proper appreciation of each one of them.

Developing the Three Skills

Skill in Meditation

You should not only learn to allow your mind to rest, you must learn to let it rest regardless of what is occurring in it. If thoughts arise, rest on those thoughts. In brief, follow the instructions given in previous sections of the text. Saraha says:

> The way to rest the mind
> Should be neither too intense nor too relaxed.
>
> Let the mind rest with clarity and without
> distraction,
> Like a lamp on a windless night.

Let the mind wander to various objects with
awareness,
Like a bird set free from a ship at sea.

Regard whatever arises in the mind as part of
mahamudra,
Like the flames of a forest fire.

Regard all sensory impressions as part of meditation,
Like reflections of the moon on water.

A yogi allows the mind to wander and rest with ease,
Like a skilful elephant herder looks after his
elephants.

A yogi should delight in sensory experiences,
Just as fields rely on water and manure.

This is the attitude with which one should meditate. This is the meditative skill you need to develop.

Skill in Preventing any Loss of Meditation

Do not worry too much about how long you can meditate or think the length of time you spend in meditation is important. All you need to concern yourself with is maintaining the proper meditative posture and practicing it correctly. Be skilled in the practice of meditation. If you gain more benefit from sitting for short but more frequent periods, you should meditate that way rather than trying to sit for long hours.

Skill in Nurturing Your Meditative Experiences Without Attachment

When you have been meditating for some time, certain meditative experiences may arise in the form of physical and mental well-being, increased mental clarity, and stability of mind. If these experiences arise, do not indulge in thoughts about them being good or bad. Simply allow yourself to have these experiences, without interpreting their significance. If you do not indulge in interpreting your experiences, they may give rise to realizations. For this reason, it is extremely important not to become attached to such experiences or to hanker after them.

The difference between meditative experiences and realization is that all meditative experiences without exception are contaminated by conceptualization. To have certain meditative experiences may nonetheless help you to attain realization, but the experiences themselves do not reveal the essential nature of the unity of experiencer and experience. When genuine realizations do occur, there will be a total unity between the experiencer and that which is experienced. The meditative experiences are bliss, clarity, and nonconceptuality.

The Meditative Experience of Bliss

This sense of physical and mental well-being is still contaminated by defilements in the initial stages, but you will gradually experience physical and mental well-being without delusions and get to a point where you experience a sense of well-being regardless of what happens to your body or mind. Nothing that happens in external situations will inflict you with emotional conflicts and your mind will be open, resilient, and clear. At this point, strange things may happen, such as thinking you have attained a high level of realization and become completely free of defilements. You may also experience a complete lack of interest in meditation sometimes. You may have a compulsion to dance and sing or make loud noises. When this state of extreme excitement is absent, you may experience the converse where your emotional conflicts and defilements appear to have increased. It may appear that the two obstacles of agitation and stupor have increased during meditation and you might feel despair at continuing with the practice. All these experiences are associated with the two sides of the same experience commonly known as bliss.

The Meditative Experience of Clarity

Your sense perceptions become more acute when you have this type of experience and you may also occasionally have certain hallucinations where you see things covered with a halo of light. You may see small circles of light bouncing off objects, or see objects covered with rainbow colors. Even when you close your eyes, your ability to picture things may be sharpened. This applies to all the senses. The mind becomes extremely lucid and awake; you do not suffer from mental fatigue or stupor and so on. You will also develop enormous confidence in your ability to grasp and understand things.

The Meditative Experience of Nonconceptuality

Having this experience means that you have developed the ability to rest the mind in whatever condition it is in. Gross conceptual activities start to subside and you are gradually able to deal with more subtle conceptual formations. Whatever meditative experiences you have, do not think of them as either good or bad. You should not give too much significance to them. There is a saying amongst meditators:

> In the summer, things grow everywhere on the ground.
> Similarly, all kinds of meditative experiences arise in the yogi's mind.

If you can refrain from indulging in evaluating these experiences, realization will definitely occur. You will realize the three kayas within the mind itself. The unceasing activity of the mind is nirmanakaya, mental clarity is sambhogakaya, and mind being empty of essence is dharmakaya. Dharmakaya is already present within you. The nature of mind is the primordially pure dharmakaya, and when you realize this, you realize the complete purity of the dharmakaya. Sometimes this is known as the "two-fold purity of dharmakaya": the primordial purity itself and the enlightenment where you actualize the dharmakaya.

Avoiding Deviations Associated with the View of Emptiness

The first type of deviation is when contemplating the nature of emptiness during meditation leads you to think it essentially does not matter what you do because everything is empty. You may think doing harmful things is not essentially harmful and cease to exercise any restraints on your behavior. This is a deviation from a real understanding of emptiness. It is important to realize that emptiness does not mean nothing has significance or there is no reality to the notion of things being acceptable or unacceptable, appropriate or inappropriate, and so on. Emptiness means that nothing has any enduring essence; it does not mean we should not discriminate between what is beneficial and what is harmful.

The second type of deviation concerns certain practices on emptiness. When you engage in meditation, you may think that you can purify all the karma you have accumulated by contemplating emptiness. You might also engage in contemplations on emptiness to improve your understanding of emptiness. There are many prescribed methods of reasoning designed to bring about a conceptual understanding of emptiness. In tantric practices, you utter the mantra of emptiness at the beginning of your visualization, saying OM SVABHAVA SHUDDAH SARVA DHARMA SVABHAVA SHUDDO HUM and then imagining emptiness gives rise to the deities and so on. Many such methods are used to bring about some understanding of emptiness, but they are all regarded as diversions in the mahamudra tradition, because they do not lead to direct realization of emptiness. All these practices of emptiness have an object, whereas in mahamudra, there is no such object. Emptiness is not seen as an object of meditation; it is to be experienced.

The third type of deviation is to become frightened that the disturbing thoughts that afflict you in meditation are preventing the possibility of your attaining liberation so that you use meditation on emptiness as an antidote. You view the disturbing thoughts or emotional conflicts as empty and try to remove them by that means. However, this is not the correct mahamudra understanding of things. Emptiness should not be used as an antidote; it should be seen as part of the disturbing thoughts and emotional conflict. They are not separate. Allow whatever experiences you have to arise without trying to suppress them and without resorting to the use of antidotes.

This is how you should avoid falling victim to deviations in relation to the realization of emptiness.

The Removal of Obstacles

The mahamudra practice of shamatha and vipashyana can positively affect your physical well-being and make you more immune to disease and illness. The different diseases that afflict human beings arise from three causes: imbalances in the psychophysical energy circulation, imbalances in phlegm, and imbalances in bile. Shamatha practice processes the *prana* or "psychophysical energy circulation," so that you become more immune to diseases arising from this source. Vipashyana practice averts diseases arising from phlegm and bile. Diseases arising from imbalances in the psychophysical energy and bile are also averted through stabilizing the mind. Furthermore, it is said that various diseases come from heat or cold, so the coolness of shamatha pacifies diseases arising from heat and the heat of vipashyana insight pacifies diseases arising from cold.

In brief, you will develop a different attitude toward sickness and ill-health. Do not regard disease and illness as an invasion of your body. Even if you become afflicted with physical ill-health or disease, regard it as the ripening of karma and have a more positive attitude towards it. Stop trying to always find some cure or other for your ill-health but instead try to work through it by changing your mental attitude. You should think, "Through the suffering I am enduring through illness, may others be free of this type of suffering." By thinking this way and developing a more positive attitude toward your ill-health, it is possible for sickness and ill-health to disappear altogether. Whenever certain crises or upsetting situations arise in your everyday life, you should try to transform them into something good. It is possible to turn a negative situation into a positive one through your response to it.

Instead of thinking that external demons or evil spirits are afflicting you with ill-health and playing with your mind, think it is your own mind that has become like a demon. All experiences of demonic possession are created by mind. They arise from disturbing thoughts. If you understand the nature of your disturbing thoughts, all the disturbing experiences arising from possession, psychosis and so on will disappear. That is the attitude you should develop to obstacles associated with bodily illness and mental disturbances.

Other obstacles to be dealt with arise in relation to the practice of meditation. As stated earlier, all the obstacles we experiences in meditation can be subsumed under the two categories of mental agitation and stupor. If your mind is agitated, try to settle it through the methods that develop stupor. If you are suffering from stupor, try to develop methods that generate agitation. In addition to the methods described in the relevant section of this text, you can do the following visualization.

Amitabha Visualization

If your mind becomes dull and susceptible to stupor, visualize Amitabha, the Buddha of Infinite Light, who is red in color, the embodiment of all the buddhas of the three times and inseparable from your own guru and the gurus of the Kagyu lineage. Imagine light radiating from Amitabha and being absorbed into your body. This light lifts all the causes and conditions of your stupor and drowsiness, such as that caused by your lifestyle, a particular situation you are in, or your own mental state. Imagine all the drowsiness that has arisen from these causes is eliminated by this light. Then imagine Amitabha dissolving into a ball of light and entering into your body so that your body is no longer the body you know. It has become a body of light, radiating from within. Your body is generating so much light that all neighboring areas in the whole of space are illuminated by it. Imagine the light extending into infinite space and then rest your mind.

Vajrasattva Visualization

If your mind becomes agitated, visualize Vajrasattva, who in this instance is blue in color. Within Vajrasattva's heart center is a blue, four-petaled lotus, from which blue light radiates. Imagine this light being absorbed into your body and dissipating your disturbed thoughts, and then rest in that state.

The obstacles of mental agitation and stupor both come from either not maintaining a proper physical posture or not creating the right state of mind. The fundamental approach for dealing with these obstacles is the practice of mahamudra, as has been pointed out in detail throughout this text. The practice of visualizations and so on are short-term methods for dealing with these obstacles, but the main method in mahamudra is to simply allow your mind to be in the state of either stupor or agitation and then trying to maintain your awareness.

The Mahamudra Path

The Four Yogas of Mahamudra

The four yogas of mahamudra deal with the path. It is generally believed that mahamudra practitioners do not need to concern themselves with the concept of a spiritual path. As Lama Shang says:

> Mahamudra is something we realize instantaneously.
> Only uneducated people feel that mahamudra
> Is related to taking a spiritual journey
> Or that its practice is orientated toward achieving a
>   certain goal.

This is true as a general statement, because mahamudra is the state of reality itself and is unchanging and undifferentiated. Since it is unchanging, we cannot speak about it in relation to time and therefore cannot use the concept of a spiritual path because that involves the notion of time and progress. However, even though this is the general understanding, we can try to understand mahamudra in relation to a path in the more specific sense of an individual's own experience. The objective reality of mahamudra does not abide in time and space, but the subjective experiences of the individual making the effort to experience and apprehend this reality can be talked about in terms of a path.

From the point of view of subjective experience,

meditators go through four different stages of spiritual fulfillment. These four stages are called the "four yogas of mahamudra." As you go through these four yogas of spiritual fulfillment, your experiences become increasingly refined, which is to say, your meditative experiences are gradually converted into meditative realizations.

The General Description of the Yogas

The yoga of one-pointedness is related to very tranquil and lucid experiences in meditation, but they are not stable and cannot be sustained for long, so they relate to meditative experiences rather than realization. We could say the experiences associated with this yoga are generally related to meditative experiences rather than realization.

The yoga of nonconceptuality is related to your experience of the nature of mind itself, because you recognize that the nature of mind is unborn and unoriginated and therefore not an entity of any kind. This understanding is also a meditative experience rather than a realization, because it is brought about by what you have heard and read rather than by direct experience, where mind recognizes its own nature through self-awareness. If such a direct recognition were to occur, that is the meditative realization of the yoga of nonconceptuality.

The yoga of one-flavoredness develops when you comprehend that the body, the mind, and the material world have no enduring essence. This comprehension is also a meditative experience rather than a realization, but if the things in the world are seen as reflections rather than as something with enduring essence, and you realize they all have the same reality even though they are independent and distinguishable from each other, that is the meditative realization of the yoga of one-flavoredness.

The yoga of nonmeditation is related to your experience

of the meditation and the meditator being one and the same. That is the meditative experience of nonmeditation because it is still the result of reflection. However, when the mind from its own side realizes meditation and meditator are nondual, that is the meditative realization of the yoga of nonmeditation.

In brief, you must always be alert to the danger of conflating these two very distinct experiences. Many meditators have fallen into the trap of mistaking meditative experiences for realization so you need to be aware of the changes that take place on each yoga as you go through these different stages. I will now explain the yogas separately and in detail.

Yoga of One-Pointedness

The yoga of one-pointedness refers to the meditator's experience of lucidity and tranquility. You are able to let the mind rest in a state of one-pointedness. The mind is not fragmented by entertaining thoughts or scattered by jumping from one thought to the next. As a result of this ability to focus the mind, there is a sense of well-being, mental clarity and a lack of the mental agitation that is usually brought about by conceptual proliferation. The yoga of one-pointedness can be divided into three stages, which correspond to the capabilities of the meditator. As you develop your ability, these experiences may last for a short time, but can gradually be sustained for much longer periods until you are eventually able to develop that meditative state spontaneously.

The First Stage

When you can allow the mind to rest without any contrivance and without trying to condition it to be tranquil, focused, and so on, you are resting the mind of its own natural accord, and all forms of gross mental agitation will subside. This experience is accompanied by the triple feelings of bliss, clarity, and nonconceptuality as the result of a reduction in your mental agitation due to reduced conceptual proliferation. Hence, you are able to remain in a state of one-pointedness. This one-pointedness may sometimes manifest after only a short time and fail to arise at all at other times no matter how long you meditate. You will not have full confidence at this point either and all kinds of uncertainties and doubts will afflict your mind. Try to develop confidence and realize that these experiences are glimpses of what can be attained through persistent practice.

As you persist with your practice, you may have a tendency to remain in the state of tranquility where there is no mental agitation. You may, in fact, develop a craving for such pleasant experiences. This is not something that should be encouraged and you should try to remain in a state of one-pointedness even with mental agitation. It is useful to think that mental agitation loses its impact if you can maintain a sense of bliss and mental clarity. Instead of fearing the mental agitations caused by conceptual proliferation will upset your mind and disturb your meditation, make an effort to maintain a sense of bliss and mental clarity while experiencing agitation. If you can maintain a positive attitude, anything that arises in your mind will not disturb your equilibrium.

This first stage of the yoga of one-pointedness is therefore about trying to apply mindfulness and awareness during meditation so that you can sustain the experience of bliss, clarity, and nonconceptuality.

The Second Stage

At this stage, the experiences of bliss, clarity, and nonconceptuality will occasionally intrude into your mind even if you are not meditating. When you do engage in formal practice, they will increase even more because of your heightened mental power. From this stage onwards, whatever experiences you have during meditation are reflected in the postmeditation situations of everyday life, because you now experience a far greater relaxation and are less inclined to react to things violently, impulsively, or mindlessly. Not only can this occur while you are awake, but also during sleep you will be less prone to harmful dreams and so forth. This is something you can distinctly experience.

The Third Stage

At this final stage of yoga of one-pointedness, meditation and postmeditation become fully integrated and you can maintain whatever experiences you have developed during meditation throughout the day. In other words, you are able to maintain the tripartite experience of bliss, mental clarity, and the absence of gross mental agitation. You will also have gained a greater insight into emptiness, which is the nature of this tripartite experience, because you realize the experiences of bliss, mental clarity, and nonconceptuality are intimately related to the nature of reality itself.

Furthermore, you realize everything you experience, perceive, and conceptualize has no distinct reality independent of mind. Mind is the key, because mind makes everything possible and without it nothing would be possible. This increased insight into the nature of mind and the reality of things means you develop confidence in what you are doing. You will also develop a certain aversion to your old way of life and old way of perceiving things, because you can clearly see the old ways were erroneous and vitiated. You can now see what your priorities are. The things you regarded as precious and indispensable are now seen as less essential and more dispensable.

Things you never thought to be important or precious now begin to assume more significance and prominence in your hierarchy of values.

Yoga of Nonconceptuality

When you are in the state of one-pointedness, your mind is in a state of mental equipoise. If you are able to remain in this state, without craving for it or becoming fixated on it, you can sustain that meditative equipoise without making an effort to develop it. You do not need to deliberately apply mindfulness or pay attention. In such a state of one-pointedness, you will come to the realization that the mind in contemplation and the mind in movement are expressions of the same nature of mind, which is indistinguishable from wisdom. You will simultaneously realize that, as far as their nature is concerned, conceptual proliferations have no origin, abide nowhere, and do not cease. The nature of conceptual constructions is revealed as the same as the nature of mind or the same as wisdom. Your experience of the world will then be altered, because your mind has become freed of the limitations imposed by the erroneous thinking of conceptual confusions.

The nature of mind, which is self-aware and luminous, becomes manifest from having shed the different layers of conceptual confusions. This self-cognizing awareness becomes nakedly present because it is now free of conceptual pollutants and you will develop the confidence that you are in charge of your own mind. You will no longer feel susceptible or vulnerable to impulses, passions, conflicting emotions, and mental aberrations, because you have realized the true nature of mind.

Unlike the previous yoga, your meditative experiences are no longer fickle and fluctuating. They become steady and established. Even if you go through various meditative experiences that you perceive as wholesome and comforting or unwholesome and threatening, you will no longer react to them in an extremely emotional way. There will be no more feelings of joy at having positive meditative experiences or reactions of fear, unhappiness, and despair about having negative experiences.

As your mind has become free of erroneous ways of thinking about the world, you will no longer see the world as having any enduring essence. Once you have developed such an understanding, conceptual categories will dissolve by themselves and you will realize the dharmakaya, which is the same as the nature of mind. In brief, the yoga of nonconceptuality is related to the dismantling of conceptual categories and constructions, which are erroneous and inhibit you from realizing the nature of mind and the reality of things. The yoga of nonconceptuality also has three stages.

The First Stage

This stage relates to the realization that reality and the phenomenal world are codependent, because the nature of the phenomenal world is reality. However, at this point, you may still occasionally lapse into old habits and old reactions in postmeditation. For example, you may become enraged if someone does something offensive or you may respond with affection if someone does something nice. Even though you know better, you may still get lured by various sense impressions from the power of habit. If you see something beautiful or hear something pleasant or see something ugly and hear something irritating, you might react in an old habitual way, instead of maintaining the higher perspective you have developed on the yoga of nonconceptuality.

The Second Stage

This stage is a more subtle experience because you still have some clinging to the idea that everything is insubstantial and without enduring essence, that everything is contingent, that nothing is absolute, and so on. You have also realized that this very mind, which is referred to as "ordinary mind," is the basis of all our experiences. All the conceptual constructions and emotional afflictions are finally and properly seen to be lacking in enduring essence. When you realize this, you are no longer vulnerable to the impact of emotions. However, it is said, even though the meditator has greater control over their emotional experiences and upheavals at this stage, he or she may still have subtle attachments to the external world. In other words, you have not yet developed proper understanding about the relationship between the phenomenal world and emptiness and there will still be some discrepancy between your meditative and postmeditative experiences. Whatever you have been able to develop and maintain during meditation may still be upset by what you encounter in the everyday world.

This yoga is realized when we gain a proper understanding of emptiness, first by realizing how our perceptions of the external world are conditioned by mind and then by realizing that mind also is devoid of enduring essence. Mind is more like space than an entity of some kind. We develop an understanding of emptiness by first understanding that what we perceive about the external world is conditioned by mind and then by realizing the nature of that very mind is emptiness. We finally come to see things as they are, without any enduring substance. The phenomenal world and emptiness are not differentiable for the simple reason that to realize the phenomenal world has no enduring essence is to realize its true nature, which is reality itself.

The Third Stage

At this stage, you are able to maintain a state of meditation throughout the day without interruptions. However, when you are asleep, you will have less control of your mind. Certain subtle forms of mental agitation may arise because you cannot maintain a state of mental clarity. It is therefore important to understand the significance of mindfulness and the importance of maintaining it. The more we are mindful and aware, the more we notice the subtle defilements and delusions that need to be purified.

The essence of all the teachings is the cultivation of mindfulness, for it is only due to mindfulness that we can refrain from reacting to things in a habitual manner. If you are not mindful, it is impossible to notice yourself doing harmful things. When you are not mindful, the mind automatically reacts to things in terms of either attraction or aversion, which gives rise to all the mental afflictions and aberrations. We develop more and more insight into the nature of mind through mindfulness and are gradually able to diminish the gross forms of delusions and then the more subtle ones. We first purify the mind of conflicting emotions and then gradually work with different layers of conceptual confusion. It is only through purifying our minds of these two types of defilement that we realize the nature of mind. As long as the mind reacts to things in a habitual way, it will be difficult to overcome the defilement of emotional conflicts. If that is not overcome, it will be impossible to overcome the defilement of conceptual confusion. As long as you believe things have some enduring essence, it is impossible to realize the nature of mind or the nature of ultimate reality.

The fundamental difference between the yoga of one-pointedness and the yoga of nonconceptuality is that you have not fully understood the implications of the nature of conceptual categories on the first yoga. However, on the level of this yoga, you realize it is not that you have to be rid of the conceptual categories so much as to realize their true nature. Once the true nature of the conceptual categories has been realized, you do not need to get rid of them as a separate act. When the nature of conceptual confusion is understood, you will realize the nature of these very confusions and the nature of wisdom are not distinct. They are the same. This additional insight comes with the realization of nonconceptuality.

Yoga of One-Flavoredness

With the previous yoga, you were concerned about dismantling your erroneous beliefs and conceptual confusions to enable a greater understanding and appreciation of emptiness. On that level, you still did not have an adequate understanding of the phenomenal world and how it relates to reality. However, due to the progress you made on the yoga of nonconceptuality, you were able to move to the yoga of one-flavoredness.

It is called "one-flavoredness" because you are no longer concerned with either understanding emptiness or trying to realize the essencelessness of the phenomenal world. You realize that all dualistic and binary concepts have the same flavor, which is the flavor of emptiness. When we speak about the phenomenal world and emptiness, relative and absolute truth, samsara and nirvana, bondage and liberation, happiness and suffering, these things always exist in a relationship for the simple fact they exist within the realm of emptiness. You are now no longer concerned with eradicating defilements or cultivating wisdom because whatever arises in the mind and the phenomenal world is perceived differently.

This ability is developed spontaneously through practice; it is not something you can manufacture through some technique. There is no technique to bring this about. This self-cognizing awareness, which has risen spontaneously, is able to perceive all things in a state of equanimity. Opposites are no longer seen in conflict, but in a complementary relationship. This experience is called the yoga of one-flavoredness and it also has three stages.

The First Stage

This is attained when you perceive things directly, so that what you perceive and emptiness is experienced as inseparable. The basic point here is that emptiness is not perceived as superior to the phenomenal world and the phenomenal world is not perceived as inferior to reality. They are perceived as complementary and having the same nature. There is also a sense of unity within the experience—body, mind, and the phenomenal world are experienced in a state of unity. It is not the case that you are in here and the external world is out there in opposition to yourself. The self, the world, and the mind are perceived in a state of total unity.

However, there is still an element of conceptual understanding involved in this experience at the initial stage. The experience is not yet completely free of certain vitiations or pollutants. You are still not fully free from influences coming from sensory impressions in postmeditation either. You might even still experience fluctuations and difficulties in maintaining total sincerity in your attitude to practice. It should be emphasized that you may encounter certain obstacles at this point. Your understanding of the complementary nature of dualistic concepts may lead you to think the efficacy of karmic cause and effect is of no real significance. This attitude may bring about a lack of concern for the welfare of others, so you should try to detect and avoid it by taking measures in advance.

The Second Stage

This stage is attained when you eliminate any notion that the perceiver and perceived are self-existing and independent of one another. Our fixation on the perceiver and the perceived as a dualistic notion is the cause of much distress, confusion, and ignorance. However, you now experience a further heightening of the nonduality of experience at this stage. You will also have fewer lapses and obstacles during postmeditation, compared to the previous stage. However even at this stage, you may still occasionally become distracted, but you will have a greater ability to bring the mind back and experience an awareness that perceives things directly in a state of unity or nonduality. You are simply aware, rather than perceiving things in terms of the duality of subject and object.

The Third Stage

You now gain the realization that everything within the realms of samsara and nirvana have their origin in emptiness and so exist in a state of equanimity. The material world and the mind are not totally distinct because they have the same nature. You are finally able to understand the real significance of emptiness through this realization. To attain the third stage of the yoga of one-flavoredness is to realize nondual wisdom. You now see the world as a magician sees his creation. Even if you have attained nondual wisdom, you will still have certain subtle obstacles that have to be worked with and may still get distracted in postmeditation. These are a few remaining obstacles to be abandoned.

The essence of the yoga of one-flavoredness is not to view things in terms of duality, but to perceive them in a state of equanimity. You no longer think certain qualities or virtues have to be cultivated and other things have to be abandoned, but appreciate the complementary nature of things that appear to be in total opposition. The importance of the phenomenal world, which was not emphasized enough on the yoga of nonconceptuality, is therefore brought back at this stage.

The fundamental difference between the yoga of nonconceptuality and the yoga of one-flavoredness is that on the former, you still did not have the ability to take whatever you perceive as complementary to your meditation and spiritual growth. You also had a certain fixation on the concept of emptiness. On the yoga of one-flavoredness, you develop the ability to use the phenomenal world, emotional conflicts and so forth as manure for the cultivation of wisdom. Whatever you perceive in the phenomenal world can be used as an extension of meditation. Sometimes this yoga is called the "path of effortlessness." However, compared to the final yoga of nonmeditation, an element of effort is still involved here. Nonetheless, we gain a proper understanding of nonduality on the yoga of one-flavoredness. The obstacle here is that we may regard meditation and nonmeditation as the same because of the ability we have developed at this stage, and think there is no need to formally engage in meditation. However, at this point, you must still persist with your meditation practice.

Yoga of Nonmeditation

Up to the point of attaining the final stage of yoga of one-flavoredness, you had not been able to eradicate certain subtle forms of defilement and obscuration. A certain element of dualistic thinking remained, along with some conscious experiences of mindfulness and some conceptual notions of emptiness. At the final stage of the yoga of one-flavoredness, all these subtle forms of defilement and obscuration were purified and you could finally realize meditation and meditator to be one and the same. When you attain the yoga of nonmeditation, you will feel a sense of well-being regardless of your experiences. Even if you do not engage in meditation, you are continuously in a meditative state and no longer need to apply mindfulness or concern yourself with distractions. Regardless of what happens internally or externally, you are in a continuous state of meditation.

There are two types of luminosity of mind: temporal luminosity and innate luminosity. Temporal luminosity is cultivated over time and is known as "son luminosity." Innate luminosity is already fully present and is known as "mother luminosity." On this yoga, the luminosity that has been cultivated and the luminosity that is innate begin to merge and become indivisible, like the ocean and its waves. The merging of these two types of luminosity produces the actualization of the dharmakaya.

Someone who has attained the stage of nonmeditation is unique and superior to ordinary human beings. Whatever that person does or thinks is always beneficial, both for themselves and for others. If that person is alone, he or she does not suffer from loneliness. Their very presence brings joy and peace to others. They are able to shed all inhibitions because they are not bound by conventional conceptual categories. They have complete confidence in expressing themselves in a sincere manner and are not afraid of judgments. Nonetheless, even this final yoga has three stages.

The First Stage

At this first stage, you are in a meditative state regardless of your circumstances or state of mind. Even in postmeditation, you will not encounter any obstacles in the form of defilements and obscurations and do not need to apply mindfulness. Even the subtlest forms of defilement, which may still be lurking around in your *alayavijnana* or "fundamental consciousness," are purified. The alayavijnana has now been transformed into primordial wisdom, because at this point, nothing is hidden. The mind is translucent, without even an element of opacity.

The Second Stage

The next stage is attained when you can establish yourself in the indivisible state of samsara and nirvana, both of which are spontaneously established in emptiness. Whatever your actions, whether awake or asleep, your mind is never vulnerable to defilement. You can maintain a meditative state even during sleep. Not only would you leave no negative karmic imprints, you would not leave any positive karmic imprints because all of your actions are unsullied.

The Third Stage

This final stage of the final yoga is attained when ordinary consciousness is transformed into wisdom consciousness. That fully fledged wisdom consciousness and emptiness become fully integrated and actualized in a state that is unadulterated, nonvitiated, authentic, and uncontrived. You have the ability to benefit yourself by actualizing the authentic state and to benefit others by actualizing the full potential of the physical body. These two abilities enable a fully enlightened being to work for the benefit of all sentient beings for an indefinite period. When meditators attain this final stage of nonmeditation, there is absolutely no difference between meditation and postmeditation, because a fully enlightened being is always in a state of meditation. This state is therefore called "nonmeditation" because there is nothing to meditate upon.

To attain this last stage of nonmeditation is to become fully enlightened. There are no defilements that need to be purified, no practices that need to be performed, no techniques that need to be applied, and no need to engage in meditation. Such a human being has become a fully enlightened one, a buddha. When meditators attain the last stage of the yoga of nonmeditation, shamatha and vipashyana have reached their culmination through the fusion of wisdom and the reality of things.

The realization of the dharmakaya is accomplished through vipashyana, which cuts through the conceptual web created by erroneous thinking and gives you the ability to benefit yourself. The realization of the nirmanakaya accomplished through shamatha gives you the ability to work for the benefit of others. A fully enlightened being engages in various physical expressions orientated toward helping and benefiting others without wavering from the authentic state of the dharmakaya. There is no time limit on how long these buddha-activities will continue and no fixed standard for how an enlightened being will engage in the practice of beneficial acts. They will apply various techniques depending on the attitudes, needs, and dispositions of others.

The mahamudra tradition says it is possible to realize this optimum state of full physical and mental potential within this very life. It is possible to develop the abilities of an enlightened being in this very body. Once you have progressed through the four stages of mahamudra, you have realized the fruition of the practice, which is buddhahood.

As a side remark, the terms mahamudra, maha ati, madhyamaka, prajnaparamita and so on refer to the same thing: ultimate reality. Ultimate reality, which is mahamudra, must be distinguished from the words and labels that are imputed on it. As far as the fundamental reality or true condition of things is concerned, it cannot be identified as this or that for the simple reason that it is not an entity. This does not mean that something about reality cannot be intimated through words and labels. They are like the example of a finger pointing to the moon. By using various techniques that are relative in nature, we can realize wisdom, because sharpening our intellect is what will ultimately lead to the acquisition of intuitive wisdom. Nagarjuna says:

> Without understanding the nature of relative truth, you will never understand ultimate truth.

Mahamudra itself is atemporal because it is not caused and it is devoid of conceptualization. Mahamudra is reality, and therefore undifferentiated. Since it is not an entity and is not caused, it does not change, has no fluctuation, and is devoid of evaluative concepts such as good and bad. This reality is not brought into being by the buddhas and it cannot be tarnished by the delusions of sentient beings. It is devoid of all the characteristics of thinghood. In brief, it is the existential condition of all things. It is all-pervasive because it pervades both samsara and nirvana. On the objective side, mahamudra is identical to emptiness. On the subjective side, mahamudra is identical to unadulterated wisdom. This unity of emptiness and wisdom is what we call "mahamudra."

If the reader feels discouraged and thinks mahamudra seems too remote from everyday experience and not is something that an ordinary person like themselves can attempt to understand, it should be pointed out that this unadulterated, nonvitiated wisdom is found within the stream of your own ordinary consciousness. It is the very consciousness that becomes agitated, confused, and performs cognitive acts. To realize nonvitiated wisdom is not to realize something other than the nature of your own consciousness. Nothing can be attained extrinsic to your own consciousness. Gampopa says:

> This very ordinary mind is not differentiable from the immaculate wisdom of an enlightened being. The mind of an enlightened being is not acquired as something new, but comes from gaining greater understanding and greater insight into the very mind with which you are already familiar.

Do not think the realization of mahamudra is related to developing or acquiring a new kind of consciousness. The very mind you already possess is also the mind of an enlightened being. Whether you have realized mahamudra or not is determined only by how much understanding you have of your own consciousness. When you have no such understanding of how consciousness works, it is called "samsara." When you gain insight into the workings of consciousness, it is called "nirvana." Even though there are various teachings of the Dharma, in essence they all point to this simple fact. Gotsangpa says:

> There is a sense of lucidity
> When the ordinary mind is left undisturbed in its natural state.
> That is mahamudra.

The mind that is unconditioned and left in its own natural state is mahamudra, because the mind that rests in its own natural state is the mind of an enlightened being. The *Sambhuta* says:

> Whether we succeed in reaching enlightenment or just become more immersed in the confusion of samsara is determined by mind. For this reason, mind is the most powerful thing. There is no other power.

Gyalwa Yanggonpa says:

> You should have a proper understanding of mahamudra or *phyag rgya chen po*. Some people say *phyag* refers to the "phenomenal world," *rgya* means "reality" and *chen* po means the "unity of the two." However, that is not a proper understanding of mahamudra; it is the understanding that you should develop in relation to dharmamudra. When the indivisibility of

luminosity, the wisdom mind, and emptiness is mentioned, this is also not proper mahamudra; it belongs to the category of samayamudra. The indivisibility of bliss and emptiness is also not proper mahamudra; it relates to the practices of karmamudra. Mahamudra proper is free from all such determinations, since mahamudra is not dependent on any kind of causes and conditions. The previous definitions are either dependent upon the experiences of bliss or lucidity and are therefore not proper mahamudra. Mahamudra is the indeterminate ground of being, upon which everything is dependent, but which itself is not dependent on anything. This is the existential condition of mahamudra, commonly called "ground mahamudra." That is mahamudra as it is in itself, without reference to anyone attempting to understand it.

Ground, Path, and Fruition

Having described mahamudra in itself, we now turn to describing mahamudra in relation to the individual practitioner. The experience of mahamudra can be understood from three perspectives: the ground, the path, and the fruition.

Ground Mahamudra

Ground mahamudra is present impartially in all things and in sentient beings. In the mahamudra tradition, an ordinary sentient being is someone who has not understood this and an enlightened being is someone who has understood this. Even though innate wisdom has been present in the depth of your consciousness right from the beginning, you have been deprived of self-realization because of "coemergent ignorance." This is not the same as an inability to appreciate a wonderful painting because it is hanging in the dark. Unadulterated wisdom cannot be objectified as something separate from your own subjective consciousness that you are unable to perceive. The eye organ may perceive things in your visual field but it cannot be the object of its own perception. You do not appreciate what is present within your own consciousness because you have been unable to gain insight into it and realize its true nature. You therefore have a misconceived notion of consciousness, in the same way that you mistake a multicolored rope for a snake.

For these reasons, your mind has been under the influence of coemergent ignorance, and you have failed to appreciate self-cognizing awareness that is wisdom consciousness. You have thereby been misled into constructing the notion of an immutable, unchanging self and mistakenly clung to this as your true identity. Craving, animosity, and ignorance develop from this clinging to a false notion of self. When your actions are motivated by these three poisons, they leave unwholesome karmic imprints on the mind, and these eventually lead to the various unpleasant experiences of samsara.

Unadulterated wisdom, which is the real nature of mind, is present within you as something totally intimate to your own being. Even though it is so close and intimate, it is also distant at the same time, because of your lack of recognition. It is like your own face. Even though it is so close, you cannot look at it.

The other obstacle that prevents an understanding and appreciation of your true nature is thinking the state of enlightenment is exalted and transcendent from your daily experiences. You have a bifurcated notion of ordinary consciousness and wisdom consciousness, which makes the two appear incompatible or that they exist in two separate realms—the transcendental and empirical realms. You can therefore miss the chance to recognize your own true nature and fail to attain realization through this lack of confidence. As long as your mind remains distracted, scattered, outwardly orientated, and not self-reflective and only used to reflect on things other than itself, it will become more and more entangled in a web of conceptual proliferation. This distraction, diffusion, and lack of self-reflection make it difficult for you to appreciate what is already present within yourself.

In brief, you should examine the ways ignorance comes into play and inhibits the realization of your own true condition. The only way to work through this is with meditation practice and proper instructions.

Path Mahamudra

This consists of cultivating the correct view, practicing meditation, and engaging in correct action. Milarepa says:

> According to mahamudra,
> Developing the correct view means nothing more
> Than cultivating a proper understanding
> Of your own nature of mind.

To develop the correct view should not be understood as the same as to acquaint yourself with subtle philosophical views on different topics. The correct view, according to mahamudra, comes from trying to develop a proper understanding of mind itself. Correct meditation is when the mind is free from the two obstacles of mental agitation and stupor. Correct action is not dictated by rules and regulations. The spontaneous act in any given situation is the correct action, because it is free from hope and fear. Gampopa says:

> When you understand that mind is luminous yet empty just like space and cease to see mind as an entity of some kind without viewing it as totally nonexistent, this is the correct view. When you let the mind rest in its own natural state and it becomes translucent, this is correct meditation. When you can act in the world without any idea of what is to be cultivated and what is to be rejected in a conventional sense, this is correct action.

Gampopa also says:

> When you develop a proper understanding of mind and its nature, this is the view; becoming acquainted with this is meditation; and acting from within this state of mind is action.

You can attain realization from developing the correct view. You can have meditative experiences from practicing meditation. The fruition of these two is buddha-activity, which is spontaneous action free from conventional constraints. Gotsangpa says:

> Understanding that samsara and nirvana are not in opposition
> Is the correct view.
> Not being overwhelmed by sensory impressions is meditation.
> Not being swayed by fluctuations in your emotions is action.

He also says:

> Your view should be free from all extremes,
> Your action should be spontaneous,
> And your meditation should be mindful.

Again he says:

> The correct view is to realize
> That the viewed and the viewer are undifferentiable.
> Correct meditation is to realize
> That meditation and meditator are inseparable.
> Correct action is to realize
> That the agent and the act are indivisible.

Rangjung Dorje says:

> Correct view comes from gaining insight into self-cognizing awareness. Correct action comes from not thinking the action and the one performing the action are separate. To do so with full mindfulness is meditation.

The essence of view, meditation, and action is the understanding that mind is the view, meditating on that without distraction is meditation, and not deviating from this is action. Tilopa says:

> Correct view comes from transcending dualistic perception.
> When the mind does not waver, it is in a meditative state.
> If one can do things without great deliberation, it is action.

Jikten Sumgon says:

> Gaining insight into the nature of mind is the view. Trying to remain consistently in that state is meditation. Acting from such a state of mind is action.

To understand these three perspectives, you need to understand the meaning of dependent origination. To understand impermanence is to understand dependent origination. To understand dependent origination is to understand emptiness. To understand emptiness is to understand the authentic state of being. Previous Kagyu masters said:

> The correct view is to look nakedly into the nature of mind.

> Meditation is remaining in that state without
> distraction.
> Action is continuously engaging in that practice.

In mahamudra, the gist of the teachings on these three aspects of practice is to realize that to cultivate the view does not mean to subscribe to a particular system of thought or philosophical tradition; it is related to immediate experience. Your meditation should be free from artificial methods of settling the mind, and your action should be free from the cultivation or abandonment of characteristics that accord with conventional norms.

Fruition Mahamudra

The fruition of mahamudra practice is attained when you actualize ground mahamudra. When you realize that ground mahamudra is inseparable from the phenomenal aspect of reality, and that reality is not separate from your everyday experience of the world, you become free from hope and fear. As mentioned in the yoga of nonmeditation, meditators develop various enlightened qualities and actualize the three kayas. They attain the five wisdoms when they transform the defilements and they attain the state of nonmeditation when the mind is totally devoid of all obscurations and defilements. In other words, when we attain fruition mahamudra, we accomplish two things: the eradication of all defilements and the acquisition of all the qualities of an enlightened being.

The way the three kayas are realized can be perceived in various ways. For example, the nature of mind that is open, spacious, and undifferentiated is the dharmakaya. The dharmakaya is revealed as a sense of openness, but it also has a sense of lucidity, which is the expression of the sambhogakaya. This mind that is empty and lucid also has the function of apprehending various things and this unceasing activity of mind is the expression of the nirmanakaya. These three aspects of a buddha's being are already present in the mind, just as oil is already present in a mustard seed. Rangjungpa says:

> The nature of mind, which is empty, is dharmakaya. The essence of the mind, which is lucid, is sambhogakaya. The activity of mind, which is unceasing, is nirmanakaya.
>
> All three aspects of a buddha's being are present within the mind itself. They also express the five wisdoms. The aspect of emptiness reveals "the wisdom of dharmata" or the wisdom that apprehends things as they are. The aspect of clarity reveals "mirrorlike wisdom." These two wisdoms coexist in a state of equanimity, which expresses the "wisdom of equanimity." Even though these two wisdoms coexist, they are nonetheless distinct, which expresses the "wisdom of discrimination." When the mind is unconditioned, these various expressions of wisdom become manifest, which is the "wisdom of accomplishment." Therefore, even the five wisdoms are inherent in the mind.

Mahamudra is realized through different methods in different traditions. In the mother tantras, the "mahamudra of bliss and emptiness" is emphasized. In the father tantras, the "mahamudra of clarity and emptiness" is emphasized. In the nondual tantras, the "mahamudra of awareness and emptiness" is emphasized. In this way, fruition mahamudra can be attained through various techniques and teachings. In addition, the tantric teachings give many kinds of *abishekas* or "empowerments" to meditators to produce various experiences of mahamudra in them. These different empowerments are designed to produce different experiences of mahamudra in terms of bliss and emptiness, clarity and emptiness and so on.

Symbolic Meanings

We now come to the symbolic meaning of the term "mahamudra." The literal meaning of *mahamudra* is simply "great seal," but the symbolic meaning can be understood by analyzing each word. In Tibet, mahamudra is called *phyag rgya chen po*. The word *phyag* stands for "wisdom," *rgya* means "this wisdom transcends defilement," and *chen po* means "wisdom and defilement are nondifferentiable" because they express a sense of unity. The *Yeshe Shepa* says:

> *Phyag* stands for "the indivisibility of bliss and emptiness" and *rgya* stands for "not going beyond that unity."

Gampopa says:

> The word *phyag* stands for "emptiness" and expresses the unoriginated nature of all things in samsara and nirvana. The word *rgya* represents the "all-encompassing nature of reality" and expresses the fact that nothing can be found that exists outside reality. *Chen po* means that "within this reality everything is self-liberated and pure," despite the fact that some things may belong in the realm of samsara and others in the realm of nirvana.

Lama Shang says:

> *Phyag rgya* basically means "not going beyond" and *chen po* represents "the all-pervasive nature of reality." The seal of a king commands authority within the boundary of his kingdom. In a similar way, the great seal of mahamudra is all-encompassing and does not discriminate between samsara and nirvana.

Khachodpa says:

> The word *phyag* means the "indivisibility of emptiness and wisdom," *rgya* means "the self-liberating nature of samsara," and *chen po* means "these two are indivisible."

Another master says:

> The words *phyag rgya* mean "the indivisibility of samsara and nirvana," and *chen po* means "all things within the realm of samsara and nirvana are included within emptiness." There is nothing more universal, more pervasive, and more expansive than reality itself.

In this way, various masters and traditional texts explain the symbolic meaning of this particular term *mahamudra*. The essence of all these quotations is that mahamudra is associated with *lhan chig skyes gyur* or "coemergence." Samsara and nirvana coemerge from reality. Sometimes it is called *phyag rgya chen po lhan chig skyes gyur*, which means "the mahamudra of coemergence." This means that, whenever we look at dualistic notions of reality and the phenomenal world or of samsara and nirvana, we realize they are coemergent. It is also called "coemergence" because of the experience we have upon realizing mahamudra—the experiences of bliss, lucidity, and emptiness that coemerge in that state. So *phyag rgya chen po* expresses this notion of coemergence.

Our experiences of virtue and vice, happiness and unhappiness, good and bad, beautiful and ugly and so on within the field of emptiness are not separable. Everything that constitutes our experience exists within the realm of emptiness, just as objects exist in space. Space does not discriminate between things that are foul and repulsive, or things that are delightful and attractive; it accommodates everything. Within the realm of emptiness, everything has the same status, the same reality. From the point of view of reality, the things that need to be cultivated and abandoned on the path and the individual who is traveling on that path all have the same nature.

If we realize that reality is all-pervasive, everything can become self-liberated. It does not matter what we experience, we have the opportunity to realize emptiness, because emptiness is present in everything. Whenever you experience something, if you realize it is empty of enduring essence and yet still an appearance of phenomena, and you can rest with that perception without any conceptual constructions, whatever you perceive will be self-liberated. It is like seeing a reflection in a mirror: we know the image is not solid and real, and yet it cannot be denied the image is there and the image is clear. In a similar way, when you realize emptiness, you realize that emptiness and phenomena are inseparable.

When coemergence is used in the context of mahamudra experience, it does not mean that two things are put together; it means that two seemingly opposite things have the same underlying nature. For example, if we look at a lump of gold, it may have three characteristics: a yellow color, heaviness, and the ability to be melted. These three characteristics have the same underlying nature, which is the gold. The very definition of gold means it must have these three characteristics, otherwise there would be no gold. We could say the nature of mind is similar. The nature of mind is emptiness, its essence is luminosity, and its unceasing activity is its thoughts and emotions, but the underlying nature of the mind is emptiness. The nature of the thoughts that arise in the mind is emptiness and the clarity of the mind is emptiness. They are also coemergent. Gyalwa Gotsangpa says:

> The Sanskrit word *mahamudra* conveys the meaning of "all-encompassingness." When mahamudra is understood as reality itself, it encompasses good and bad, beautiful and ugly, spiritual and nonspiritual, because everything exists in its own perfection. If a thought arises in the mind and is left alone, coemergent wisdom can arise from that very thought.
>
> Whether you realize this to be true or not, the very nature of the thought is inseparable from its true condition. That is the symbolic meaning of *phyag rgya*. When a particular thought becomes self-liberated, it becomes undiluted wisdom.
>
> The wisdom consciousness of an enlightened being is not found elsewhere; that is the meaning of *chen po*. This all-encompassing reality, which pervades both the mental and nonmental realms, can be called mahamudra, coemergence, madhyamaka, or dzokchen. Whatever word we use, there is no conflict in essence.

Phagmo Drupa says:

> The nature of reality is devoid of the extreme notions of existence and nonexistence, so it corresponds to the madhyamaka view. Reality cannot be fully expressed

> in language, so it is in keeping with the teachings of prajnaparamita. Everything is perfect within its own natural condition within the realm of reality, both in terms of samsara and nirvana, so it is in keeping with the views of dzokchen. In reality, nothing is intrinsically evil or intrinsically good, so it is in keeping with the views of the mahamudra teachings. To understand that reality is all-pervading and that there is no need to abandon defilements because they can be used to enhance your spiritual practice is in keeping with the teachings of tantra.

There is no conflict between whatever system of teachings we may use, because ultimately we are trying to realize and understand the same reality, whether we call it madhyamaka, prajnaparamita, dzokchen, coemergence, or mahamudra.

E-Vam Institute

E-Vam Institute in New York seeks to foster the study and practice of the Kagyu and Nyingma lineages of Tibetan Buddhism in the West. E-Vam Institute works to promote understanding between the Buddhist traditions and the other major faith traditions in the world as well as to bring greater understanding between the various Buddhist schools and lineages themselves.

E-Vam Institute in New York
171 Water Street
Chatham, NY 12037
Phone: 518-392-6900
E-mail: office@evam.org
Web: www.evam.org

Kagyu E-Vam Buddhist Institute
673 Lygon Street
Carlton North, Vic, 3054
Australia
Phone: 61-3-9387-0422
Email: office@evaminstitute.org
Web: www.evaminstitute.org

Nyima Tashi Kagyu Buddhist Centre
20 Williamson Avenue
Grey Lynn
Auckland, NZ
Phone: 64-9-361-2305
E-mail: nyimatashi.nz@gmail.com
Web: www.nyima-tashi.org.nz

Yeshe Nyima
49 High Street
Harris Park, NSW 2150
Phone: 61-2-9893-9008
E-mail: yeshenyima@live.com.au

Books by Traleg Kyabgon

The Influence of Yogacara on Mahamudra
KTD Publications, USA, 2010

The Practice of Lojong: Cultivating Compassion through Training the Mind, Shambhala Publications, USA, 2007

Nyima Tashi: The Songs and Instructions of the First Traleg Kyabgön Rinpoche, translated by Lama Yeshe Gyamtso
KTD Publications, USA, 2006

Mind at Ease: Self-Liberation Through Mahamudra Meditation, Shambhala Publications, USA, 2004

Essence of Buddhism: An Introduction to Its Philosophy and Practice, Shambhala Publications, USA, 2001

May all beings be happy!

We express our gratitude and appreciation to Traleg Kyabgon Rinpoche for his kindness and support in the production of this book; to Dee Collings and all at E-Vam Institute in New York for all their help and cooperation. We thank Chris Tucker for his excellent copyediting and Basia Coulter of BasiaDesign for the beautiful layout.

Maureen McNicholas and Peter van Deurzen

KTD Publications, a part of Karma Triyana Dharmachakra, is a not-for-profit publisher established with the purpose of facilitating the projects and activities manifesting from His Holiness's inspiration and blessings. We are dedicated to "gathering the garlands of the gurus' precious teachings" and producing fine-quality books.

KTD Publications Wooodstock NY www.KTDPublications.org